17.50

41669

Production Management for Film and Video

Production Management
for Film and Video

Richard Gates

FOCAL PRESS

Focal Press
An imprint of Butterworth-Heinemann Ltd
Linacre House, Jordan Hill, Oxford OX2 8DP

 PART OF REED INTERNATIONAL BOOKS

OXFORD   LONDON   BOSTON
MUNICH   NEW DELHI   SINGAPORE   SYDNEY
TOKYO   TORONTO   WELLINGTON

First published 1992

© Butterworth-Heinemann Ltd 1992

British Library Cataloguing in Publication Data
Gates, Richard
    Production management for film and video.
    I. Title
    791.43068

ISBN 0 2405 1332 0

Library of Congress Cataloguing in Publication Data
Gates, Richard.
    Production management for film and video / Richard Gates.
    p. cm.
    Includes index.
    ISBN 0 2405 1332 0
    1. Motion pictures–Production and direction. 2. Video
    recordings–Production and direction. I. Title.
    PN1995.9.P7G38   1992
    791.43'0232–dc20   91–33088
                                                    CIP

Composition by Scribe Design, Gillingham, Kent
Printed and bound in Great Britain by
Biddles Ltd, Guildford and King's Lynn

CONTENTS

PREFACE

It is usual for books of instruction to be full of rules on how to do this and how not to do the other and, in this respect, this book follows the tradition by proposing that there is one golden rule for the production management of films and that is that there are no golden rules.

However, there are some strong business guidelines which need to be followed if a production is to reach a successful conclusion. These guidelines have nothing to do with the art of programme-making but everything to do with the business of programming. Therefore the purpose of the book is to try and give the basic information needed in order to manage the production of a film or programme from start to finish in the most efficient and effective way possible.

In order to cover the wide range of options that are opened up by the different problems presented in the production management of films and video productions as varied as features, documentaries, advertisements, animation and pop-promos, this book will concentrate on the kind of productions which could be considered to represent either end of the film-making spectrum. By looking at what is required for the production of a feature, at the top end, and a documentary, at the bottom end, it is expected that most of the problems and solutions for the management of a film or programme will be covered on the understanding that most productions will fall within these two extremes. This is not to say that documentaries are always less complex than feature films or that feature films have to be difficult to make.

The one kind of production that falls outside the usual form of production is the animated film, in that the organization of the shoot is a different process although many of the basic production principles still apply to the whole programme making process and particularly so in the pre-production period.

The one caveat that should be remembered is that the detailed information in this book should not be regarded as gospel because every production is original and therefore has to be treated individually. It must be realized that every film is a prototype and the guidelines which follow should be altered to meet the needs of the particular production requirements of the programme or film being made. What works for one production may not be valid for another. This is particularly true in the practical differences between film and video production. The reasons for choosing one or the other medium will be in the hands of the producer and director. Much of the production management will be the same for either format but an appreciation of the differences between the two is essential.

The management of a production, like any other field of business which concerns the management of people, combines the skills of distinguishing between what is practical and impractical, what is necessary and unnecessary, and then persuading those who have to execute the production decision to do so. It is the marriage of these two skills, the correct evaluation of the job and the motivation of the personnel, which is the essence of good production management.

This book is intended to explore the first of these skills. Namely, how to decide what is practical and necessary for a production, and this hopefully will provide a guide for students who wish to be involved in production management or, if they are already involved, want to improve their expertise.

The other side of the business, that of personnel management, is a vital one for the smooth running of any industry, particularly one where artistic temperaments may clash. Detailed consideration of these skills are outside the scope of this book although some aspects of managing crews and casts may be touched on where they affect the practicalities of production.

Also outside the scope of this book is the role of the producer, though sometimes it will be touched upon because an understanding of their work is required to enable the individuals responsible for the management and running of a production to perform their business effectively.

Production management is about the business of programme-making, and it must be realized that the art of film and the business of production have to accommodate each other; *the Production Manager has to be aware of the weight of the creative requirements, the Director has to adjust to the business limitations*; only when this happens will the making of a film or video have the chance to proceed smoothly.

In a way similar to Louis B. Mayer's reply to Joseph L. Mankiewicz's request to be allowed to direct when Meyer said 'No, you have to produce first, you have to crawl before you can walk', so it is hoped that this book will be a guide on how to crawl more efficiently around all the skills needed in production management.

ACKNOWLEDGEMENTS

A book of this nature cannot be written without the help of many people who know their part of the film industry far better than I could ever hope to.

I would like to thank the following people who gave me their time and expertise while I was writing this book.

Peter Robery of Ruben Sedgewick Insurance Services for advice concerning the intricate world of film insurance, on which he and they are experts.

Barry Measure of Samuelson Film Service London and The Grip House, together with Hugh Whittaker of J.D.C. Ltd., for their invaluable assistance and deep knowledge regarding the business of hiring equipment.

Ernie Marsh of Warwick Dubbing Theatre for his comments on the re-recording process, based on his long experience.

Eddie Dias of Michael Samuelson Lighting, for information on hiring lights and generators.

Paul Oliver of Lee International Studios, Shepperton for explaining how a good studio, like Shepperton, can help a production manager.

Ted Shorthouse of Colour Film Services Group for comments on the laboratories' point of view.

Pete Dimbleby of Agfa-Gaevart Ltd., for information from the film manufacturer's point of view.

Brian Shemmings of the ACTT for clarifying some points regarding the Unions and the role they play in the industry.

Shirley Leavis of Samfreight Ltd., for the information about carnets and transporting productions.

John Adams of the Department of Drama at the University of Bristol.

Andrew Webb of Lee Lighting Ltd.

Martin Amstell of the London International Film School.

Paul Collard of Metrocolour London.

Ron Rogers of Colour Film Services Group.

Andrew Patrick of The Producers Association.

Julia Heddon of the Mechanical Copyright Protection Society.

Shirley Northey of the Performing Rights Society.

Channel 4 Television Ltd for the reproduction of some of their budgeting documentation.

Finally I would particularly like to thank Alain Silver, an experienced American producer who gave me invaluable advice from the American point of view, Jake Wright, a production manager with wide experience, and Stuart Lyons, a producer with extensive knowledge. All these colleagues read my manuscript at various stages, and besides making constructive improvements they gave me much encouragement during the writing of this book. My appreciation for their help is unbounded.

Also my thanks go to my editor, Margaret Riley, without whom this book would never have materialized.

CHAPTER 1

THE PRODUCTION MANAGER

In the film world it has been said that if you earn money it is an industry but if you lose money it is an art form.

Whatever the truth of this assertion regarding films, and the industry as a whole, there can be no doubt that for every production there is the business of making the film or programme and this is the business of the production manager.

It is the job of the production manager, to run or manage the production. This means that the production manager has to ensure that all the material that is needed for a production is available, from the most exotic location to the street around the corner, from the largest set to the smallest prop, and this material is available at the right times, at the right place, in the right amount and at the right price, and that everyone knows what is expected of them.

There is no direct artistic input in this process—it is simply the business of management—but a well-managed production will give the creative talents the time and consequently the opportunity to express themselves and for this reason creative talents should appreciate the work of a good production manager. Equally, a production manager should realize that his or her actions and decisions will have an effect on the artistic process of a production even if this is not immediately apparent.

The work of a production manager will vary with the size and scope of a production.

The need for a production manager on a feature film is obvious. The crew is large and consequently more specialized and the business of organizing and coordinating all these individuals is clearly important. The need to ensure that the whole team is working together and is happy in its work should be self-evident, but in a climate of different creative talents and often very dominating personalities (choose the directors you love to hate) it should be realized that this is not an easy job to do. In addition to the size of the crew, a feature film will usually require a large quantity of equipment and many other services all of which have to be brought together at one time, and this is the responsibility of the production manager.

On the other hand, the producer of a documentary, with a shooting crew of eight or nine, very often will do the work of a production manager. It is a common practice on independent documentary productions for a director to instigate the production and consequently become the producer/director of the project. When this happens it should be realized that there comes a time on the production when the producer/director can no longer do efficiently all that needs to be done, even on the relatively simple production of a documentary. Consequently a production manager should be appointed and this appointment should start well before the planned shooting date. Within the documentary discipline there have been films where production assistants, particularly when they are very experienced, have run the production. Although they have continued to hold the title of production assistant they are essentially managing the production and therefore are in all but name the production manager.

These then are the two extremes of complexity of production: the feature at the expensive end and the documentary at the economic end of the financial scale. Most productions fall between these two poles; commercials are generally regarded as 1 or 2 day features, pop promos are a mixture of feature and documentary and can be almost anywhere on the complexity scale, and drama documentaries can range from being close to features down to using straightforward documentary techniques.

A word of caution is in order for those who feel that the feature film is the only place where proper film making is done. It should be realized that this is not so. Indeed the excitement and challenge of production managing a documentary comes from being involved in all aspects of the production whereas working on a feature, particularly a very big feature, may result in the production manager's role being much closer to industrial management.

To understand this management role it has to be understood that the production manager is the executive head of the production department, and all the other departments, art, camera, sound, editorial and music, should refer to the production department for strategic and financial guidance. In turn the production manager refers to the producer and director for approval of the production department's plans with regard to the financial and artistic requirements of the production.

Thus, looking at the position of the production manager in terms of a family tree the relationships are usually as shown in Figure 1.1.

It can be seen from this 'family tree' that the production manager, together with the producer and director, is one of the key members of a production and generally will be involved in the project from start to finish, or should be. This is why the production manager's job is so exciting. The production manager has the satisfaction and fun of seeing the film grow from its early days and develop through all the stages until it is completed. This also means that he or she is more directly involved in the pain of when things go wrong and gain pleasure from the successes when they are achieved.

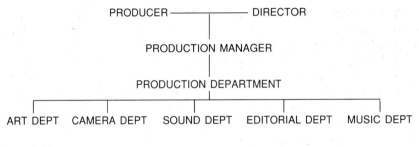

Figure 1.1

In order to appreciate where this pain and pleasure may come from it is necessary to understand the main steps required to get a production from its beginning through to completion and delivery.

Some comment also needs to be made about actions taken after delivery. These activities are not the responsibility of the production manager, but knowledge of them should increase understanding of the importance of the duties undertaken by the production manager during filming.

CHAPTER 2

THE PRODUCTION PROCESS

An understanding of the basic structure of a production, from the start to the finish, is needed in order to realize what has to be done at any one moment in the making of a film because if this understanding is not there time will be wasted in pursuing the wrong requirements.

In simple terms this means that time should not be spent worrying about hiring an editing room or dubbing theatre if the locations have not been sorted out or the crew or equipment has not been hired. A production has a logical order and this needs to be followed if a successful conclusion is to be achieved.

So what is the first step?

THE IDEA

The idea. No idea, no film.

The idea may come from many sources but the people who are most frequently involved are the producer or the director or the writer or some combination of these three. In essence, whoever initiates the idea is the producer and this person may continue with the idea themselves to become the actual producer or they may collaborate with someone who is a recognized producer, this being the way most writers and some directors proceed.

A production manager would not expect to be involved at this stage but the way a project develops has an effect on the extent of involvement of all the crew in a production and particularly a production manager.

Having got the idea the next step is to decide what kind of project is to be developed. This means that the idea has to be evaluated.

THE EVALUATION

The evaluation of the idea is done in terms of the likely cost of the project, the likely source of funding for the proposal and the likely market.

The size of the budget will almost certainly determine where the finance for the idea will come from. However, the kind of project and potential market may determine the limits of the budget.

It can be seen that these two factors of budget and market are related and consequently have an effect on each other. There are some specialized production agreements which allow those films which fall within their scope to be made at lower costs. A feature film outside these low-budget agreements begins at a cost of 1½ million pounds sterling and can go up to almost any price. For example, the recent film *Baron Munchausen* cost a reported 48 million US dollars. The original budget was apparently $24 million, which, if true, means the production went 100% over budget. There have been other productions equally well known for their high costs, but even a budget of the generally considered modest sum of 1½ million pounds sterling is usually outside the financial constraints of a television company and consequently the producer will be looking to those companies which finance features for funding.

On the other hand, documentary films, which usually have budgets in the range of £40 000–50 000 per half hour, are seldom funded by the major studios and generally expect to receive their money from television, although it should be noted that a documentary series may well begin to reach the budgetary levels of a small feature.

So if the kind of project has a bearing on the likely budget available and source of finance to be tapped or if the size of budget affects the kind of project that can be contemplated it can be seen that any factor which has an effect on the possible budget has a bearing on the project. Therefore a major factor in the evaluation is the proposal's likely market as this may help determine the possible returns the film is likely to earn and consequently the size of budget which can be accepted with a realistic profit still to be made.

Having evaluated the proposal in terms of cost, funding and eventual market the next step is to develop the project.

THE DEVELOPMENT

The development of an idea consists of two elements: the raising of the finance and the actual developing of the project. Essentially this is the stage where the idea begins to be turned into a reality and this reality will usually be in the form of a script synopsis or outline proposal; it is also the first hurdle for the project. This is also happening while the project is still under the producer's wing, but a good producer will be looking for assistance from all parts of the industry.

If you have a couple of Oscars under your belt you can probably get the necessary finance to start a feature without having a detailed development but if you do not have such a track record you will need a full script and draft budget, so a production manager may well be called in at this time. A production manager working at this stage will not necessarily expect to be involved in the eventual production and probably will be contracted only to do the initial work to get the proposal off the ground. Therefore a feature producer is going to need some finance to pay a writer to write the screenplay and a production manager to calculate a budget, so a source of development funding has to be tapped in order to get to the stage where a project can be presented to potential backers.

With a documentary, depending on its subject, scope and style, the producer is less likely to require a fully written script but he or she will still need a fully prepared proposal together with a draft budget in order to give the backers an idea of what the project is and what it is likely to cost. Because the eventual budget is less than for a feature, the funding for development is also less; indeed in most cases the money will come from the producer's own pocket.

Having got the idea to a stage where it can be presented to backers the producer has reached the next stage in the production process.

PRODUCTION FINANCE

Raising production finance is often the longest and hardest part of any independent producer.

For example, it took Richard Attenborough more than 10 years before he eventually got *Ghandi* on to the screen and this kind of timescale is by no means rare. Another example is Jane Fonda's *Old Gringo* which she had been involved in developing for 8 years. Yet both these producers have good established track records.

There are a number of reasons for the delays. Sometimes it is politics. Oliver Stone's film *Platoon* was eventually financed through a British-based company because no American financier wished to be associated with what was felt to be a potentially sensitive subject. Sometimes it is the cast. For example the right person may not be available: David O. Selznick had to do a special deal with MGM to get Clark Gable for *Gone with the Wind* and this was before he had found Vivien Leigh to play Scarlett O'Hara. Sometimes it is the subject matter. If the financiers are not convinced the film will be successful then they will not put up the money or they may remove their backing at a crucial moment, which means that the producer has to start all over again. Twentieth Century Fox took *Star Wars* off their slate at one stage because they did not believe that space movies would be popular. So, having got to this stage in the production, it should be realized that there are a lot of hurdles still to be surmounted and problems to be overcome.

Depending on the size of the production, a full-time production manager may or may not be employed at this stage; on features the expected answer would be yes but on documentaries the answer is probably no, unless it is a long series. Again a production manager may be employed to prepare further budgets for the production without any extended commitment, an action which should be understood in the light of the protracted development process.

An understanding of why this period is such a protracted one and sometimes so difficult is useful. Essentially the reason is quite simple. The backers, whoever they are, will not hand over the money without detailed contracts and a clear idea of what is being proposed and this usually means extensive negotiations. These negotiations may well involve a lot of people, financiers, stars, writers, directors and the producers, not to mention the cooperation of outside bodies, like the Indian government during the production of *Ghandi*. All of these people have to agree and the agreement has to be noted; indeed it is a good policy to get everything written down before a production begins to roll whatever the size of the production. Although the production manager will not be involved in most of the negotiations, it is important that they are aware of what has been agreed, and is even better to set an agreement down in writing. When Samuel Goldwyn said 'A verbal contract isn't worth the paper it is written on' he was expressing a universal truth for all production managers.

Therefore, even if a backer has agreed to finance a production the standard advice is do not believe it until the contract is signed and even then many features still have not reached the screen. Once television companies have agreed to fund a film they will almost certainly do so, but again a contract has to be signed. In both cases it must be remembered that the financiers are buying something before it is made, so they want to be as sure as they possibly can that they will get what they are promised. One of the ways they do this is to hand the money over at agreed stages of the production, usually a third on signature of the contract, a third on the commencement of principal photography and the final third during the post-production, a production fee being paid on delivery.

Thus one of the duties of the producer or production manager will be the calculation of a cash flow forecast. On a larger production this may well require the involvement of a production accountant.

It should be realized that for feature productions it is usual to form a company, limited by guarantee, to execute the particular production, and television companies which commission independent productions also only deal with limited companies even at the documentary end of the scale. The backers will want to be sure that the money is properly accounted for, so, at the bare minimum, a separate account should be opened even if a separate company is not formed for the production. Whatever the contractual terms for the financing of the production the day will finally come when the money is deposited in the film company's account and from this moment on the practical business of production can begin. This is the pre-production stage.

PRE-PRODUCTION

In a sense every stage up to this one is part of pre-production but, depending on the size of the production, all these stages could have been completed by one individual, and on documentaries sometimes are.

However, in the case of a feature, a producer will certainly need the assistance and advice of a lawyer, possibily an accountant and/or a banker as well as the director, writer and other key production personnel.

Once the money is in place the key production personnel will be engaged and the pre-production period for the shoot begins in earnest. The staff contracted at this stage will be the heads of departments with the production manager as the link between them and the producer and director. At the same time the production office has to be established.

It is at this stage that the production manager's skills in evaluating the priorities for the production come into play and they are most obviously required in the process of budgeting and scheduling the film.

BUDGETING AND SCHEDULING

For the production manager budgeting and scheduling are the beginning of the production proper and it is important that the estimations made at this stage be as true as possible. However it is as well to bear in mind that, the only time a production manager can be sure of the schedule or the budget is the day after the film is delivered; up to that time things can happen which may result in changes having to be made.

The details of how budgets and schedules are drawn up will be dealt with in Chapters 9–11. Both these types of documents are derived from a breakdown of the shooting script and on a feature or any other drama production the cross-plot is produced during this stage.

At the same time as the budgeting and scheduling are progressing the next major stage should also be beginning and this is the business of casting and crewing the film. It must be realized that in the case of a major feature the principals, or stars, will probably be in place already, as well as some of the key technicians. This is because the financing of a major feature often depends on whether there are any major 'names' in the production.

CASTING AND CREWING, LOCATIONS AND STUDIOS

Casting is fairly straightforward.

The choice of cast will be made by the director and the producer with the help of a casting director and the cast covers everyone, including stunt artists, who is involved in performing in the film. Stand-ins may well come with the contracted stars but if this does not happen they and the crowd artists will probably be auditioned by the assistant director in consultation with the director.

The crew depends on which agreement the production is being made under. Thus feature films have to have a minimum of twenty BECTU members employed although it is very rare for a feature to be able to be made with less. Documentaries are usually crewed to need but would usually expect to have at least a director, production manager, camera person, camera assistant, production assistant, sound recordist and electrician, or sparks as they are known, on a shoot.

The crew list shown in Figure 2.1 is that which might be required for a feature film or filmed television series under The Producers' Alliance for Cinema and Television (PACT)/Trades Union (TU) agreements. The majority of the crew will be members of the Broadcasting Entertainment Cinematograph and Theatre Union (BECTU).

Although this is a basic list of technicians and staff and their unions which are likely to be used on a feature film, the actual requirements of the individual production will determine who and how many will be needed and for how long they will be contracted. The factors which decide these matters will have been determined from the budget and schedule. These factors will be considered in the following chapters.

Just as the cast and crew have to be engaged as early as possible, so do the locations and studios. Finding a location is only part of the job because, once it is found, the location manager needs to get the necessary permissions for the production to take place there and, depending on the location, this may result in a number of lengthy negotiations. A studio, if it is required, also has to be booked as soon as possible because other productions may be wanting to use the same facility and a production manager does not want to have the film's schedule determined by the availability of studio space.

Before the shoot finally goes ahead there is one important meeting that has to take place, as follows.

THE PRE-PRODUCTION MEETING

The pre-production meeting is between the relevant unions and the production company, usually represented by the producer and production manager. The unions in the UK are the BECTU, EEPTU, MU and Equity. The purpose of the meeting is to ensure that all agreements will be observed by all the parties and that the production company is in a financial position to honour its commitments to the crew it has contracted to work on the production. In return the unions agree to honour their obligations to the production company.

Once a pre-production meeting has been satisfactorily completed the production should be in a position to proceed.

THE SHOOT

The production management practicalities of this part of the making of a film will be dealt with in Chapters 13 and 14. However, the production manager's responsibilities will extend beyond the basic business of running the production. There are a number of other people who will

ADMINISTRATION

Producer
Production supervisor
Production co-ordinator
Production assistant
Researcher
Secretaries to above and clerical staff

Associate producer
Production manager
Production accountant
Publicity director

PRE-PRODUCTION/CONSTRUCTION

Supervising art director
Draughtspersons
Location finder
Supervising dress designer
Casting director
Set dresser/Decorator
Property hand
Construction manager
Supervising chargehand
Engineers
Painters
SFX supervisor
Miniature SFC
Stagehands
Electricians – EEPTU
Standby fireman
Advance rigger/Scaffolder

Art director
Scenic artist

Costume designer

Production buyer
Upholsterer/Drapes

Chargehand
Carpenters
Plasterers
SFX technicians
Model makers

Plumbers

Basic rigger/Scaffolders

MAIN SHOOTING LIST

Artists – EQUITY
Stunt personnel – EQUITY
Director
2nd Assistant director
Script supervisor (Continuity person)
Lighting cameraperson
Follow focus
Key grip (Senior grip)
Grip
Sound mixer
Location manager
Stills photographer
Gaffer (Chief electrician) – EEPTU
Electricians – EEPTU
Make up
SFX (special effects) personnel
Specialist personnel (pilots, armourers, etc.)
Drivers

Crowd artists – FAA

1st Assistant director
3rd Assistant director

Camera operator
Clapper/Loader   Video operative
Dolly grip (responsible for tracking)

Boom operator   Sound maintenance

Unit publicist
Best boy (Senior electrician) – EEPTU

Wardrobe   Hairdressers

CATERING UNIT (usually contracted out)

Chef

Canteen staff

SECOND UNIT

Camera crew, sound crew and production crew as needed

POST-PRODUCTION

Supervising editor
1st Assistant editor
Dubbing editor
Dubbing mixer
2nd Assistant dubbing mixer
Sound camera operator
Projectionist
Music editor
Musicians – MU

Editor
2nd Assistant editor
Assistant dubbing editor
1st Assistant dubbing mixer

Sound maintenance

PROCESSING (not engaged directly by the production company)

Laboratory technicians

Figure 2.1

visit the set and these will include the backers, publicity, health and safety personnel, the unions and sometimes fans or other friends or hangers-on. All these people have to be controlled and catered for so that the filming can proceed smoothly.

The completion of the shoot will mark the end of the involvement of the majority of the technicians and only the editorial crew and production office will expect to be involved beyond the shooting period.

EDITING

Once the shoot has finished the filmed material must be organized; this is the editing process.

Although the pressure may be eased at this time there is still the possibility of the production facing a tight delivery date and consequently the completion schedule may put the editorial crew under considerable pressure.

There are a number of elements which have to be organized, scheduled and controlled, for editing is more than sorting the footage into its final order. There is the sound, and the need to record any special sound effects or re-record or dub any dialogue. There are special optical effects which, in films like *Star Wars*, may take longer to achieve than the original shooting. There is the music as well as the many other items which may be required, like library material, and all these have to be scheduled. One of the key elements in the post-production schedule is the booking of a dubbing theatre. This needs to be done as soon as possible because, as with studios, other films will be wanting to use these facilities and good dubbing theatres will be booked well in advance.

The organization of these elements is the responsibility of the editor, although in consultation with the production manager the editor will define the needs of his or her team in order to complete the editorial process. Part of this process is the incorporation of music in the film.

MUSIC RECORDING

Music is an important ingredient of any film but is too often overlooked, especially on lower-budget productions. The mechanics of the music recording is the responsibility of the music director and the production manager.

If the production is having music specially recorded for the film then there will be one, or more, recording sessions. The music director, like the heads of the other departments, will be recommending who should be employed and where the recording should be done but it is the production office which will be arranging the details and contracting the musicians who work on the basis of daily or session chits. Therefore the production manager needs to be aware of the particular requirements for

MECHANICAL-COPYRIGHT PROTECTION SOCIETY LIMITED
Licensing Department

Elgar House, 380 Streatham High Road, London, SW16 6HR

01-769 3181-9

SPECIMEN MUSIC CUE SHEET

TITLE OF FILM, VIDEOTAPE, SLIDE PROGRAMME OR VIDEOCASSETTE..

PRODUCER (Name and address—Telephone No.)...

SPONSOR (if applicable)..

TYPE OF RECORDING (film, videotape, sound tape to accompany slides, videocassette, etc.)...........................

EXHIBITION (Whether paying audiences, non-paying audiences, cinema advertising,
television programme, television commercial, etc.)...

TERRITORY OF DISTRIBUTION...

DETAILS OF MUSIC USED:

DURATION Mins. Secs.	DESCRIPTION OF USE i.e. whether Instr. or Vocal; Visual or Background accompt.	TITLE OF MUSICAL WORK	COMPOSER	PUBLISHER
	(The musical works used should be set out under the above headings.		Given below are a few specimen entries).	
2 12	Instrumental Background	March of the Bowmen from 'Robin Hood' Suite	F. Curzon	Hawkes & Son (London) Ltd., O.2042.
2 03	*Vocal Visual	Land Of Hope And Glory	Edward Elgar	Sir Edward Elgar Will Trust/Booses & Co. Ltd.
23	Vocal Background	Mother's Little Helper	M. Jagger/K. Richard	Mirage Music Ltd., Decca SKL 4786.
14	Vocal Visual	Never Ending Song Of Love	D. Bramlett	United Artists Music Ltd.
1 58	Instrumental Background	New Generation	Silvio/Cortley	De Wolfe Ltd. DW/LP 3160A.
2 27	Instrumental Background	Original Music, Specially Composed	J. Neville	Ms.

*A 'Visual' use is one which is part of the production and is deemed to be heard by or performed by any of the characters in the film.

It is necessary to obtain prior permission before any recordings are made. Where music is dubbed from a Gramophone Record the Manufacturer's name and the number of the record must be given.

L/IL

Figure 2.2

musicians. If music is bought 'off the shelf' then again the production office will be involved in sorting out the clearances required, so the production manager should have some understanding of what is required.

At the completion of the editing and music recording stages the results have to be put together and this is done at the mix, or final dub, as it is also known.

THE MIX

Like most of the processes in the production of a film the mixing of the soundtrack appears to be a simple operation but, without proper preparation, it can easily go astray.

As it is part of the editorial process the mix usually is managed by the editor but as it is also part of the production the production manager must be on hand to ensure that the editor is receiving the back-up required. On the editor's advice the production office should book the dubbing theatre, ensure that any looping cast are available, confirm that equipment or material for special sound effects is to hand and generally make sure that time is not wasted in the dubbing theatre through lack of planning.

The crew of a dubbing theatre has a lot of expertise to give to a film but, in common with individuals involved in all the other areas of a production, it can only give of its best if it has been informed of what is expected.

Besides the producer, director and editor, the only other crew member at the mix should be the sound recordist/mixer. This is not always possible with freelance staff but good management, if not courtesy, should mean that the recordist is invited.

On completion of the mix the film should be ready to be returned to the laboratories for the final print to be produced.

THE PRINT

The production of the print is the penultimate stage in the creation of a film and, as far as the production office is concerned, the preparation needed is similar to that used for the dubbing process.

The laboratory used for the final print has to have all the material in its possession, that is the cut negative, the soundtrack, the titles and any other special effects material which may have been produced outside the laboratory's own walls.

Again the producer, director and editor would expect to be at the viewing of the answer prints, and the director of photography or lighting camera person should be invited to these viewings. An early stage of the production of the final print is the grading of the negative which requires the assistance of the director and the lighting camera person.

On a feature film the heads of departments would expect to be present at any stage which affected their department but, as noted above, because of budgetary restrictions this is not always possible.

With the acceptance of a final answer print the laboratory should be in a position to deliver show prints. The production has now reached a stage where it can meet one of the key points negotiated during the financing of the project, that is the delivery date.

Depending on the end user, the contract will also specify in what form the production has to be delivered and for television programmes this will generally mean a video tape rather than film. Modern laboratories provide transfer services and they should be consulted at an early stage to determine the best way to put the programme onto tape. This does not mean that a married print is not wanted. Festivals generally prefer to show film and often it is easier to transfer from film to tape than from one tape format to another tape format. All these are Producer's decisions but they have to be executed by the Production Manager.

DELIVERY

The delivery is essentially the end of the production for the editorial crew but the producer and the production office still have work to do because delivery is more than handing over a copy of the film or videotape.

This part of the production process will be examined in detail in Chapter 16.

While details for the completion of the delivery are being pursued by the production manager the producer will probably be involved in the next stage—the promotion and publicity of the film.

PROMOTION AND PUBLICITY

At this stage the production manager will no longer expect to be directly involved in the production, but clearly the business of promotion and publicity will have been in progress throughout the whole of the production and the production manager needs to be aware of these requirements.

The publicity staff need to be given access to the shoot, the performers and information about the film so that the audience can be made aware of the forthcoming event. At this stage the producer and distributors will redouble publicity efforts to give the film a strong send-off.

EXHIBITION

The exhibition or showing of the film is the culmination of all the work.

The producer needs to be sure that the film is seen, otherwise there will be no financial return and, as indicated earlier, the film business is about money.

Finally, the producer has to consider the delightful or daunting prospect of money coming in or going out.

ONGOING COSTS? ONGOING INCOME?

The question of whether or how a film makes money is the business of the producer and essentially beyond the scope of this book, but it should be remembered that a well-managed production which comes in on budget is in a better position to recoup its costs and that the control of the production depends on the competence of the production manager.

CHAPTER 3

A FEATURE SCRIPT
(First few minutes)

'You need three things for a good film and they are the script, the script and the script!'

A Hollywood saying

There was an occasion when John Ford was shooting a film and on one day, while on location, a couple of the front office executives arrived on the set and asked to speak with Ford. In the consultation that followed they explained they they were very concerned because the production was 3 days behind schedule and the front office wanted to know what Ford was going to do about the situation. Ford called for an assistant to bring a copy of the script. 'Three days?' asked Ford, and the executives confirmed the estimate, so Ford counted out nine pages of script which he tore from the rest of the screenplay and then handed these pages to the executives with the comment 'Right, we're back on schedule.' The executives were then invited to return to their office and let him get on with his work.

The sequel to this incident occurred a short while later. Some of the screenwriters in Hollywood were upset at the cavalier way in which Ford had used the script, so Joseph Mankiewicz, then head of the Writers' Guild, sent Ford nine blank pages and invited him to 'direct this script'.

There cannot be enough emphasis on the importance of the script; it is the blueprint by which a production is guided.

Clearly no script, no film.

Regrettably this fact is too often overlooked by the inexperienced director or producer and not appreciated by the other technicians involved on the work. The need to understand this point is particularly true for the production manager because it is from the script that all the information for the subsequent planning is obtained.

A production manager is unlikely to be involved in choosing a script but may be involved during the production of the shooting script and certainly will be involved once the shooting script has been completed. Therefore it is important to realize the difference between the original script or screenplay and the shooting script.

The original script is a literary document which the producers and financiers can assess. A shooting script is a technical document for the use of the crew and should be clearly labelled as such. It is good policy for the production manager to oversee the publication of the shooting script and decide on the allocation of scene numbers, scene headings and other technical details.

There is a tendency for inexperienced film writers to present shooting scripts which detail every shot. This is not wanted and consequently is a waste of effort. The person who reads the script wants to read the story, not the instructions on how it is to be made. If writers hope to direct their own work they should not need to tell themselves how they are going to shoot it, and if the script is presented to an independent director the chosen director does not want to be told how to shoot the film. So on all these counts and particularly the latter one, a shooting script should not be the first stage.

Individual directors have individual styles and one of the stylistic trade marks may be in the way the film is cut. The editing of a film can range from a cut every few frames to films with no or almost no cuts in at all.

The classic example of an 'uncut' film is Alfred Hitchcock's *Rope*. Yet the completed production has all the usual range of wide-angle and close-up shots in it. The Hungarian Miklos Jansco is another director who uses long tracking shots rather than repeated cutting and gains the effect he requires by moving closer or further from his subject by movement rather than cutting. Thus the script as interpreted by a director like Jansco will show the production manager what kind of shot is required and therefore what technical requirements will be demanded in order to achieve this shot.

Figures 3.1–3.4 on pages 18 to 28 represent the first few minutes of a feature script entitled 'WIZARD'. It is the opening of the film and this example will be used as the basis for the other production disciplines required in the management of a feature production.

Pages i and ii show the traditional way a script is laid out. The notes on the next three pages, iii, iv and v (Figure 3.2), show how a director might think of shooting this particular screenplay.

From these notes a shooting script may be produced. This is not a necessity but if it is produced it may look something like Figures 3.3 and 3.4, and this information will be the first step towards a detailed breakdown of the project. At this stage every shot will be numbered. This can be done in various ways. The most obvious is to begin at one and continue through the script until the end is reached (Figure 3.4). An alternative method is to number the shots in the individual scene and put these numbers after the scene number. This has the advantage that a shot in the middle of the script can be more easily found.

Whatever method is used the important point to remember is to be consistent throughout the production.

Figure 3.5 shows that even after a shooting script has been prepared there will still be additional information to be recorded.

In addition to providing the primary information for a breakdown the shooting script is needed so that a cross-plot can be drawn up, a schedule worked out and the continuity monitored. It will be seen from the above example that the information needed by a production manager for organizing the production can be extracted only from the details provided in a shooting script.

Also, it should be noted that some of the shoots may form part of the same set-up. For example in Figure 3.5, shots 6.3, 6.5, 6.7 might be done as one set-up, just as the two close-ups on Melanie, 6.6 and 6.8, could also be dealt with together. The production manager, together with the first assistant director, must know for certain what the director wants from these shots because there is a big difference between the time needed for two set-ups and five.

If the script is the blueprint for the production then the shooting script is the equivalent of the detailed plans and it is from these plans that the quantities and costs are calculated. The details of how these items are calculated will be considered in the following chapters.

However, it must be realised that the shooting script should not be such a detailed straight-jacket that it inhibits all spontaneity in the actual shooting. This means that allowance has to made for a margin, and sometimes a considerable margin, of variation in any Director's shot list. How these variations are accounted for will also be considered in the following chapters.

WIZARD

TITLE SEQUENCE

A crystal ball hangs in space. It floats on one side of the screen and the titles roll up the other half. As the titles finish a landscape appears in the crystal ball and we take a closer look at what is to be seen.

The TITLE SEQUENCE ends and we dissolve through the ball into:

1. EXT. NORTH DEVON COUNTRYSIDE—DAY

The North Devon countryside. A grubby looking estate car is driving through the lanes on a grey day. The car is very modern by today's standards, but as we are some time in the future it is quite old. The driver is Dr RICHARD FAIRFAX and with him is his daughter, MELANIE, who is in her early teens. She protests as they drive.

              MELANIE
But you promised.

              RICHARD
I did?

              MELANIE
Yes. You said if it was wet we'd go and see a film.

              RICHARD
Ah, yes. Well it's not wet, is it?

              MELANIE (*frustrated*)
Oh Daddy! It's been raining all morning.

              RICHARD
But Pussy Cat, it's not now, is it?

              MELANIE
Don't call me that!

              RICHARD
But I thought you liked it.

i

Figure 3.1

This comment is met with silence. RICHARD FAIRFAX is an archaeologist. He wears old tweed jackets, cord trousers and rimless glasses. He is good looking but totally unconscious of the fact because his overriding passion is his work. MELANIE is dressed in the current fashion and will soon be a stunning-looking woman. She appears to be very confident, but for all her occasional outward bravado she still clings to her childhood and particularly a large and at one time brightly patterned canvas shoulder bag, into which she puts all the things she cares about.
After a while RICHARD tries to placate MELANIE.

                    RICHARD
    Anyway, I won't be long.

                    MELANIE
    You always say that when you go on one of your smelly digs.

                    RICHARD
    Now Mel, you know that's not true.

                    MELANIE
    What about the last time? Why can't you be like Uncle Chris?

                    RICHARD (*exasperated*)
    Last time was an accident. Ah, we're here.

It begins to drizzle as the car goes over a small bridge which leads to the site of an archaeological dig. The bridge crosses a small stream which runs alongside the site of the dig.

                                        CUT TO
2. EXT. CAR PARK AT THE SITE OF THE DIG — DAY

The car comes to a halt in the small park near the site. RICHARD gets out enthusiastically but MELANIE remains inside looking fed up. The rain has stopped.

                    RICHARD
    I won't be long. Why don't you go for a walk?

                    MELANIE
    I don't want to.

                        ii

Figure 3.1 *continued*

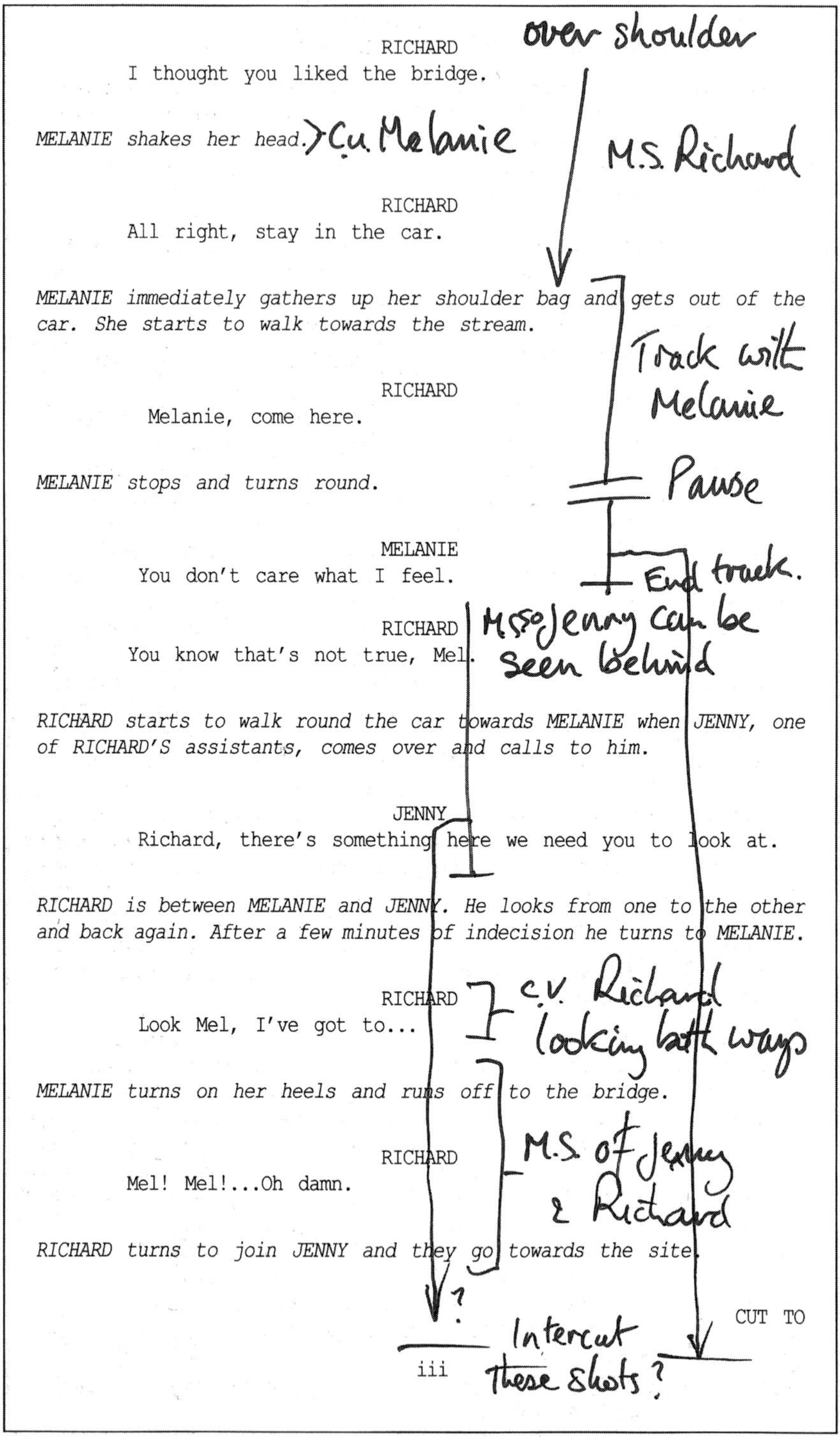

RICHARD
I thought you liked the bridge.

MELANIE shakes her head. >C.u. Melanie

over shoulder

M.S. Richard

RICHARD
All right, stay in the car.

MELANIE immediately gathers up her shoulder bag and gets out of the car. She starts to walk towards the stream.

Track with Melanie

RICHARD
Melanie, come here.

MELANIE stops and turns round.

Pause

MELANIE
You don't care what I feel.

End track.

RICHARD
You know that's not true, Mel.

M.S. Jenny can be seen behind

RICHARD starts to walk round the car towards MELANIE when JENNY, one of RICHARD'S assistants, comes over and calls to him.

JENNY
Richard, there's something here we need you to look at.

RICHARD is between MELANIE and JENNY. He looks from one to the other and back again. After a few minutes of indecision he turns to MELANIE.

RICHARD
Look Mel, I've got to...

C.V. Richard looking both ways

MELANIE turns on her heels and runs off to the bridge.

RICHARD
Mel! Mel!...Oh damn.

M.S. of Jenny & Richard

RICHARD turns to join JENNY and they go towards the site.

CUT TO

iii

Intercut these shots?

Figure 3.2

3. EXT. UNDER THE BRIDGE NEAR THE SITE - DAY

MELANIE is sitting under the bridge. By her side is her shoulder bag. In her lap is an old teddy bear and she is reading a paperback book (Anne of Green Gables). She re-reads a passage, then puts the book down and looks up. She has been crying and she doesn't look very happy. She rummages in her bag and pulls out a mirror and some lipstick. She looks in the mirror. She gets a tissue and wipes the tear stains from her face then she tries the lipstick. It is not a successful effort so she wipes it off. She looks round. It has clearly stopped raining and a break in the clouds allows the sun to shine brightly. MELANIE packs her bag, gets up, and moodily walks along the bank of the stream.

slow track out with M. between camera CUT TO

4. EXT. FIELDS NEAR THE SITE - DAY *track along with M. and stream   hold on flash*

As MELANIE walks she notices a very bright reflection off an object on the other side of the stream. She crosses the stream to investigate and finds a crystal globe in the muddy bank at the edge of the stream. It has been revealed by the water of the stream washing the dirt from its surface. c.u. globe — c.u. Mel *She picks the globe up and, after cleaning it, looks into it. As she does so, she sees the face of a young man looking back at her. She drops the globe in fright. She looks round but sees no* c.u *one is near, so tentatively picks the globe up again. She looks* Mel *again and the face of the youth is still there. The young man is MERLYN. He is in his late teens.* uncle in *The face smiles and mouths the words 'Follow me'. Again she drops the globe but this time from surprise rather than fright.* wide *She squats and picks the globe up for the third time. This time when she looks the young man is* C.U. *further away and beckoning her to follow. She can see that he is dressed in Celtic garments covered by a cloak. MELANIE looks up* wide *to see if she can see where the young man is but there is no one in sight. She looks at the crystal again. The figure is still* C.U *there beckoning so she goes in the direction indicated as she recognizes the landscape in the background.* wide angle with trees in background CUT TO

Quick cuts

→ C.U.s of M. and wide of reactions

5. EXT. A TREE-COVERED HILL NEAR THE SITE - DAY

The crystal globe leads her to the edge of a small clump of trees on a low rise. In the middle of the trees there is a circular stone sheep pen, and beyond the pen can be seen a single standing stone on the top of another low hill. Pan round at end of Track *The figure of MERLYN in the crystal leads her to a part of the* M.S *wall which is highlighted and indicates that she should pull one* Mel *of the stones from this section. When she does so, a hole behind* look *the stone reveals a lead box with runic devices on it.* round *MELANIE doesn't know what to do with the box so looks to the* wool *globe for guidance, but now nothing can be seen except an inverted image of the area. She holds the globe in different lights, but the image of MERLYN has disappeared.*   wide shot

M.S. of Mel C.u of action and c.u. of Mel inspecting box. Find. c.u. of Globe iv over shoulder POV of wall

From ends of trees tracking to wall

Figure 3.2 *continued*

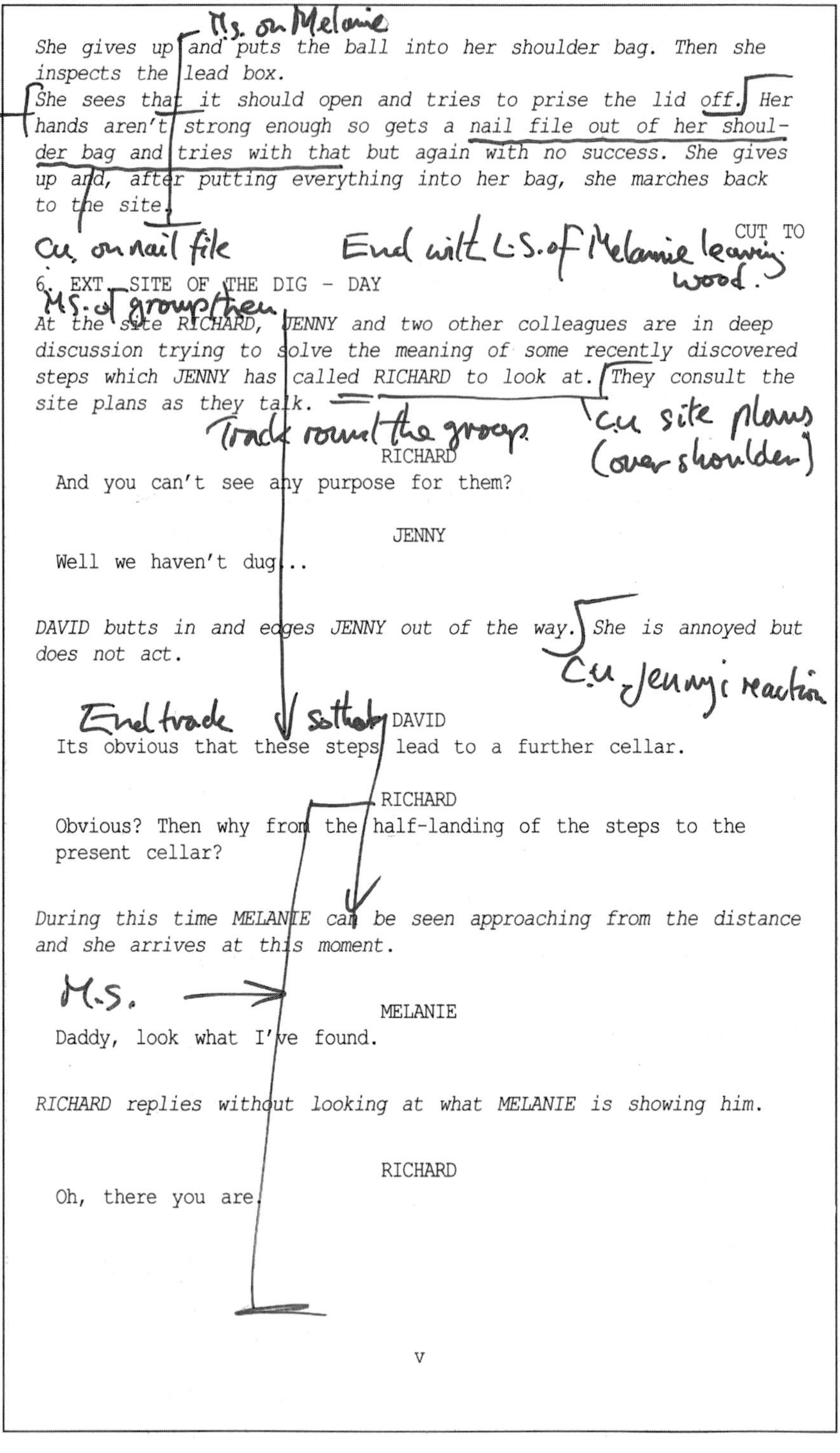

She gives up and puts the ball into her shoulder bag. Then she inspects the lead box.

She sees that it should open and tries to prise the lid off. Her hands aren't strong enough so gets a nail file out of her shoulder bag and tries with that but again with no success. She gives up and, after putting everything into her bag, she marches back to the site.

CUT TO

6. EXT. SITE OF THE DIG - DAY

At the site RICHARD, JENNY and two other colleagues are in deep discussion trying to solve the meaning of some recently discovered steps which JENNY has called RICHARD to look at. They consult the site plans as they talk.

RICHARD

And you can't see any purpose for them?

JENNY

Well we haven't dug...

DAVID butts in and edges JENNY out of the way. She is annoyed but does not act.

DAVID

Its obvious that these steps lead to a further cellar.

RICHARD

Obvious? Then why from the half-landing of the steps to the present cellar?

During this time MELANIE can be seen approaching from the distance and she arrives at this moment.

MELANIE

Daddy, look what I've found.

RICHARD replies without looking at what MELANIE is showing him.

RICHARD

Oh, there you are.

v

Ms. on Melanie
C.U. on Box
C.U. on nail file
End with L.S. of Melanie leaving wood.
M.S. of group then
Track round the group.
C.U. site plans (over shoulder)
C.U. Jenny's reaction
End track so that
M.S.

Figure 3.2 *continued*

6.6 - C.U. Melanie.

> MELANIE
> Daddy! ...

6.7 - L.S. of group.

> RICHARD
> Well what is it?

MELANIE thrusts the lead box in front of RICHARD but his atten-tion is on the plans and not her.

> RICHARD
> Yes Mel, very nice.

6.8 - C.U. Melanie

> MELANIE
> You never...

6.9 - M.S. Track back with Melanie until Jenny catches her.

MELANIE turns away and stamps off in anger. JENNY looks after her and then follows. RICHARD is totally unaware of what he has done to upset MELANIE. JENNY catches up with MELANIE.

> JENNY
> Melanie, can I see what it is?
> MELANIE
> Why?
> JENNY
> Please.

MELANIE gets the box out of her bag and hands it to JENNY. At first JENNY casually looks at it but then begins to realize the importance of what she has.

6.10 - C.U. Jenny.

She glances towards the other archaeologists, then back at MELANIE.

6.11 - M.S. Jenny and Melanie.

> JENNY
> Oh my...! I think your father should have a proper look
> a this.
> MELANIE
> No. Its mine.
> JENNY
> But Melanie.

MELANIE sticks her hand out and JENNY reluctantly returns the box.

vi

Figure 3.3

MELANIE

Only if I show him.

JENNY nods agreement ...

6.13 - M.S. Track back with Jenny and Melanie, end with pan onto Melanie.

and they go over to where RICHARD is, the discussion having broken up.

JENNY

Richard. I think you had better have a proper look at what Melanie has.

MELANIE is smiling.

CUT TO

7. EXT. THE ENTRANCE OF THE GREENHAM HISTORY RESEARCH INSTITUTE — DAY

7.1 - M.S. Tracking and pan as car turns into gate.
RICHARD'S car drives up to a large security gateway with a barrier across it. The sign by the gate states 'Greenham History Research Institute - M.O.D. Property - No unauthorized admittance - All passes to be shown'. Opposite the sign at the other side of the gate is a statue group representing the Greenham Common Women. RICHARD is driving the car. JENNY sits beside him with MELANIE in the back. A guard checks who they are and then the barrier is raised to let them through.

CUT TO

8. INT. THE SECURITY OFFICE AT THE GREENHAM H.R.I. — DAY.

8.1 - C,U, on machine and track back to M.S. of room.
RICHARD has just passed through the X-ray machine and JENNY is about to go through. MELANIE is waiting her turn and stands next to the security desk. A SECURITY GUARD turns to her.

SECURITY GUARD

Your bag please miss.

8.2 - M.S. Melanie and Guard.

MELANIE

What for?

SECURITY GUARD

We have to check it.

8.3 - C.U. Melanie looking up at Guard.

MELANIE

Why?

vii

Figure 3.3 *continued*

8.4 - C.U. Guard.

                              SECURITY GUARD
          Please miss, can we just check your bag.

8.5 - C.U. Melanie.

                                MELANIE
          Why?

8.6 - C.U. Guard.

                              SECURITY GUARD
          You can't go in unless we do.

8.7 - M.S. Over Guard's shoulder looking down on Melanie and across the rest of the room - so we can see Chris's entrance.

                                MELANIE
          Why?
                              SECURITY GUARD
          Miss...

At this moment unnoticed by MELANIE Professor CHRIS WATSON, who is a large, jolly looking, bearded man, comes up behind her.

                                CHRIS
          Can't take orders as usual I see.

MELANIE spins round with a cry of delight while the SECURITY GUARD looks on stony faced.

                                MELANIE
          Uncle Chris!

CHRIS gives her a big hug and at the same time notices' the SECURITY GUARD'S face.

                                CHRIS
          No not you. This young lady.

8.8 - M.S. The three of them from one side.

CHRIS unwraps himself from MELANIE and pushes her back to the security desk.

                                CHRIS
          Now, show the man the contents of your bag, then we can
          get on.

MELANIE looks at CHRIS then begins to do as instructed. The SECURITY GUARD doesn't give the crystal globe a second glance.

                                                            CUT TO

                                viii

Figure 3.3 *continued*

9. INT. CHRIS WATSON'S OFFICE IN THE GREENHAM H.R.I. - DAY

74 - C.U. on box then track across to show the others and the room.
The lead box is on a table under a very bright light. The table is at one end of a very modern but functional room. At the other end of the room seated on some comfortable chairs are MELANIE, RICHARD and JENNY. CHRIS is seated behind his desk and MELANIE is explaining to 'Uncle Chris' where she found the box. She is still smiling broadly.

MELANIE
... so I had a look under the stones and there it was.
CHRIS
Well it certainly is quite a find.

CHRIS gets up and goes over to the table to have another look at the find.

CHRIS
There's one thing I still don't quite understand.

75 - M.S. on Richard then pan to Chris.

RICHARD
What! Only one thing?

CHRIS ignores RICHARD

CHRIS
What made you look there?

76 - C.U. Melanie.

MELANIE
Where?

77 - C.U. Chris.

CHRIS
At those stones. ... I mean had you noticed them before?

78 - C.U. Melanie.

MELANIE
No.

79 - C.U. Chris.

CHRIS
So?

80 - C.U. Melanie.

MELANIE just shrugs her shoulders, she isn't smiling now.

81 - M.S. Chris - track with him when Andrew comes in.

CHRIS is watching her carefully and is puzzled by her evasiveness.

ix

Figure 3.4

                              CHRIS
                Well you can't have just...

*At this moment there is a knock on the door and ANDREW, a senior
technician, comes into the room. In his hand he has a thick
folder containing various prints of the scans done on the box.*

                              ANDREW
                Professor, I've got the scan results here.
                              CHRIS
                And?

Track towards Chris's desk.

                              ANDREW
                There's definitely something inside but we don't know what
                it is.
                              RICHARD
                What's it look like?

ANDREW hands the file to CHRIS then turns to RICHARD.

                              ANDREW
                That's the problem. We can't get a picture of the con-
                tents.

82 - C.U. Chris.

CHRIS looks up from studying the photographs, he smiles.

                              CHRIS
                So, it looks as if we have no option. As they used to
                say, we'll just have to 'open the box'.

83 - Wide over Chris's shoulder at the rest.

The others look totally bemused at CHRIS'S comment.

                              CHRIS
                Never mind. Only history. Richard, will you and Jenny take
                the prize along to the lab, Andrew will show you the way.
                Mel and I will be along in a minute.

84 - Wide shot tracking in on Chris when he begins to speak.

*CHRIS busies himself with papers while RICHARD collects the lead
box from under the lamp and follows JENNY and ANDREW out of the
office. CHRIS starts talking with MELANIE while he continues sorting papers.*

                              X

Figure 3.4 *continued*

                                    CHRIS
        So, how's the boyfriend?
                                    MELANIE
        I don't have a boyfriend.
                                    CHRIS
        Oh, *boyfriends* is it?
                            MELANIE (*disgusted*)
        No.
                                    CHRIS
        You surprise me. I would have thought...

Track ends about here. Hold on Chris.

                                    MELANIE
        Not with the choice at my school.
                                    CHRIS
        Ah. So what led you to find it?

85 – C.U. Melanie.

                                    MELANIE
        Led me?

*MELANIE is caught off-guard by the question. CHRIS stops sorting
his papers and watches her.*

86 – C.U. Chris.

                                    CHRIS
        Yes, led...if you'd said you'd been playing around and
        knocked the wall over and then seen the box, well – that
        I would have accepted, but your story implied that you
        were led.

87 – C.U. Melanie.

MELANIE looks at the floor.

88 – Two shot of Melanie and Chris.

                                    CHRIS
        Don't you trust me?

MELANIE looks at CHRIS.

                                    MELANIE
        You won't laugh?

                                    xi

Figure 3.4 *continued*

5.8 - M.S. of Melanie.

She gives up and puts the ball into her shoulder bag then picks up the lead box. She looks at it and seeing that it should open she tries to prize the lid off.

5.9 - C.U. on hands.
5.10 - M.S. on Melanie.

She fails with her hands so gets a file out of her shoulder bag and tries with that but again with no success.

5.11 - C.U. on file.
5.12 - L.S. on Melanie, pan round to follow her out of wood.

She gives up and, after putting everything into her bag, she marches back to the site.

CUT TO

6. EXT. SITE OF THE DIG - DAY
6.1 - M.S. of Richard and colleagues talking.

At the site RICHARD and three of his colleagues are in deep dis-cussion trying to solve the meaning of the recently discovered steps which JENNY had called RICHARD to look at.

6.2 - Over the shoulder C.U. of the plans.
6.3 - L.S. Track round group.

They are consulting the site plans as they do so.

> RICHARD
> And you can't see any purpose for them?
> JENNY
> Well we haven't dug...

DAVID butts in and edges JENNY out of the way.

6.4 - C.U. Jenny's reaction.
6.5 - L.S. of group and end track.

She is annoyed but does nothing.

> DAVID
> It's obvious that these steps lead to a further cellar.
> RICHARD
> Obvious? Then why from the half-landing of the steps to the present cellar?

During this time MELANIE can be seen approaching from the distance and she arrives at this moment.

> MELANIE
> Daddy, look what I've found.

RICHARD replies without looking at what MELANIE is showing him.

> RICHARD
> Oh, there you are.

v

Figure 3.5

6.6 – C.U. Melanie.

> MELANIE
>
> Daddy!...

6.7 – L.S. of group.

> RICHARD
>
> Well what is it?

MELANIE thrusts the lead box in front of RICHARD but he is now concentrating on the plans and not her.

> RICHARD
>
> Yes Mel, very nice.

6.8 – C.U. Melanie.

> MELANIE
>
> You never...

6.9 – M.S. Track back with Melanie until Jenny catches her.

MELANIE turns away puts the box in her bag, and stamps off in anger. JENNY looks after her and then follows. RICHARD is totally unaware of what he has done to upset MELANIE. JENNY catches up with MELANIE.

> JENNY
>
> Melanie, can I see what it is?
>
> MELANIE
>
> Why?
>
> JENNY
>
> Please.

MELANIE gets the box out of her bag and hands it to JENNY. JENNY carefully looks at it at first but then begins to realize the importance of what she has.

6.10 – C.U. Jenny.

She glances towards the other archaeologists then back at MELANIE.

6.11 – M.S. Jenny and Melanie.

> JENNY
>
> Oh my ...! I think your father should have a proper look at this.
>
> MELANIE
>
> No. It's mine.
>
> JENNY
>
> But Melanie.

MELANIE sticks her hand out and JENNY reluctantly returns the box.

vi

Figure 3.5 *continued*

MELANIE

    Only if I show him.

6.12 - C.U. Jenny.

JENNY nods agreement ...

6.13 - M.S. Track back with Jenny and Melanie, end with pan on to Melanie.

... then moves over to where RICHARD is, the discussion having broken up.

JENNY

    Richard. I think you had better have a proper look at what Melanie has.

MELANIE is smiling.

CUT TO

7. EXT. THE ENTRANCE OF THE GREENHAM HISTORY RESEARCH INSTITUTE - DAY
7.1 - M.S. Tracking and pan as car turns into gate.
RICHARD'S car drives up to a large security gateway with a barrier across it. The sign by the gate states 'Greenham History Research Institute - MOD Property - No unauthorised admittance - All passes to be shown'. Opposite the sign at the other side of the gate is a statue group representing the Greenham Common Women. RICHARD is driving the car with JENNY beside him with MELANIE in the back. A guard checks who they are and then the barrier is raised to let them through.

8. INT. THE SECURITY OFFICE AT THE GREENHAM H.R.I. - DAY
8.1 - C.U. on machine and track back to M.S. of room.
RICHARD has just passed through the X-ray machine and JENNY is about to go through. Melanie is waiting to go through and is next to the security desk. A SECURITY GUARD turns to her.

SECURITY GUARD

    Your bag please, miss.

8.2 - M.S. Melanie and Guard.

MELANIE

    What for?

SECURITY GUARD

    We have to check it.

8.3 - C.U. Melanie looking up at Guard.

MELANIE

    Why?

vii

Figure 3.5 *continued*

CHAPTER 4

A DOCUMENTARY PROPOSAL

The difference between a documentary film and a feature film is generally clearly recognized. The two kinds of production can come together in the form of the drama documentary but as this usually is a dramatization of factual events, the basis of the script being dictated by history rather than imagination, this kind of production generally follows the same pattern of production as for a feature film or other drama production.

The documentary is a different type of production and, in its classic form, is intended literally to be a document of what happened in front of the camera.

In passing it should be noted that all documentaries are biased, as indeed all productions are, but it is only those programmes which have a political or other sensitive content which may present a problem for the programme maker and consequently for the production manager, particularly in the latter stages of production where the requirements of the commissioning body may result in alterations being asked for at a time close to the delivery date. Therefore it is doubly important for the scope and content of a documentary to be clearly understood by all parties at the beginning of the production in the hope that this will reduce or negate the likelihood of editorial problems arising; hence the need for detailed negotiations and written agreements.

There are a number of different styles for documentaries, each of which has an effect on the way they are made and therefore their likely cost and schedule.

The oldest of these is the 'fly on the wall' as exemplified by films like Flaherty's *Nanook of the North* and Grierson's *Man of Arran*, but even these films had a degree of direction in them. In recent years there have been television documentaries like *The Family* which have tried to eschew detailed direction, although in reality this is not always possible. The most obvious effects that this style of filming has can be seen in the kind of equipment used, particularly lighting, and the quantity of film shots, ratios of 30:1 or more being used. The shooting crew will be minimal but the editorial crew will have to be expanded just to deal with the quantity of footage.

The 'wildlife' documentary, probably the most popular and universal kind of production and often the work of dedicated individuals, presents production problems of its own. The business of getting to the locations, the time spent waiting for the animals to perform, the specialist knowledge needed to find the subjects and the resources used to create the right environments all have to be considered by the production manager. For example, the producers and crew of the feature documentary *Blue Water, White Death* had to travel half-way round the world to find their quarry, the great white shark, and were very close to running out of money before their 'star' appeared. Obviously there was very little any of the crew could do to improve the situation under those circumstances. However, there are companies which are able to create the right environments for the subjects to be photographed in and thereby save the long, risky and uncertain business of trying to catch the subject in the wild.

A common ploy in the 'wildlife' documentary as well as other forms of documentary production is to have a 'voice-over' commentary. This is a useful style for programmes which incorporate difficult concepts which require explanations that cannot be given by pictures alone. The benefits for the production from this kind of presentation are that the detailed script can be written after the shooting and made to fit the visuals. Probably one of the most consistent kinds of this type of production is the 'industrial documentary', which is a film made by a company with the intention of promoting some aspect of its business or activities. Two of the reasons for choosing this style of filming are its economy and the potential for making late changes to the script depending on the material shot or the information needed to be imparted.

A similar form of production uses a presenter to provide the links and explanations between individual parts of the programme, some of which may be in 'voice-over'. Both types of documentary allow the director, and consequently the production manager, some control over the production in terms of content and schedule. The director will always determine the eventual content of a film, but in the cases of 'fly on the wall' or 'wildlife' documentaries very often the content can only be chosen from the material available, whereas other styles of production can give directors a greater scope for imposing their own ideas on the material and this means that the production manager will have more responsibility for controlling the production.

The last style of production and probably the cheapest form of documentary programme, which has developed because of the financial constraints of television, is the 'talking head' documentary. Broadly speaking this kind of programme consists of individuals being interviewed about the subject of the documentary and these interviews make up the majority of the programme. The reason why this form of production is so inexpensive can be realized when considering what makes up the cost of a production.

If, for example, a programme is made by recounting the events of some historical occurrence it is much easier to find some witnesses to the event and film them in a controlled environment, often their own home, talking about the event. The time taken to set up, film an hour of interview and depart will almost certainly be no more than a morning or afternoon and may be as little as a couple of hours. Therefore if two interviewees are filmed each day and 5 minutes from each interview used in an eventual half-hour programme, it should readily be appreciated that 3 days is all that is required to complete most of the half-hour production. As crew costs are one of the major budget items in a documentary production, it can be seen that the 'talking head' documentary is potentially a cheap form of programme making.

The nature of the documentary film, excluding the drama-documentary form, means that there seldom is a detailed script for the production. This is because it is impossible to know what precisely is going to happen when the cameras roll. The result is that the majority of documentaries are commissioned on the basis of a proposal. The more detailed this document is the better the production office can establish the parameters for the production.

In the presentation of a documentary proposal the style of production should be summed up in the treatment. How the production is to be filmed, or treated, gives the production manager a clearer idea of the likely schedule for the film and therefore the likely budget for the film.

Because documentary programmes are often made with small crews it should be realized that a documentary producer may be directly involved in the work usually performed by a production manager. What is being considered here are the duties that are the responsibility of a production manager regardless of whether a particular person is appointed to the post or whether a member of the team developing the production, usually the producer, eventually does the work.

PREPARING A PROPOSAL

To understand the factors that have to be considered when evaluating a documentary it is helpful to understand how a proposal might be put together for presentation. Figure 4.1 shows an example, each stage of which is described below.

Firstly, the cover of the proposal document should state the title of the programme, what the proposal is for, the date of the proposal, who is presenting it and their address. It should be realized that television companies receive hundreds of proposals and that a particular one may become separated from the accompanying covering letter; therefore the proposer's name must be attached to the proposal document.

The next page may well be an index. This is useful as an indication of the documents which make up the proposal.

The subsequent pages should describe the body of the proposal and should include a 'proposal' which defines what is planned, a 'treatment' which defines how it is to be realized, a 'synopsis' or an 'outline' of the structure for the programme, which may be a draft script, a budget (the business of budgeting will be dealt with in more detail later in the book), and finally an appendix which includes any additional information relevant to the proposal.

It will be noted that the proposal states that the programme is to be half an hour long. In reality, depending on the contractor, the programme is generally less than 30 minutes long because of the requirements of advertising and/or continuity but as these requirements vary from country to country and station to station there is little benefit in trying to match individual specifications. The eventual contract will determine if the half an hour is in reality 26 minutes and 20 seconds and the hour is to be 52 minutes and 40 seconds or some other length.

For a series there will be the need for a page or pages to indicate what is going to be covered in each programme and this is part of and an extension to the proposal.

The appendix should contain any information which is material to the production but not directly needed for the understanding of how the project is to be executed. For example, letters granting permission for the production to film in particular locations or letters from people the production wishes to interview agreeing to the request.

In Figure 4.1 the proposal is for a documentary series and page 3 outlines what is being proposed. From the production manager's point of view the key words on this page are in the last sentence and these are, 'We are proposing that each of these programmes be thirty (30) minutes in length and that they be shot on videotape.' This gives us the length of each programme and format. A different project could propose three programmes of 45 minutes in length shot on 16 mm film or any other combination of time, format and number of programmes. The important fact is to know what is being proposed.

The next page defines more clearly what the proposal is to cover but this is of no immediate concern for the production office.

Page 5 covers the treatment and will indicate the kind of film or video production being planned. This should give the production manager further details of the possible problems to be faced in the production. The key words here are 'will be shot in a studio setting', 'an actor', 'stylized study or library', 'will incorporate a chroma-key screen' and an 'actor playing the . . . anchor-man'. This treatment shows the production manager what will be wanted in terms of cast, location and equipment for the programme.

A proposal for a single documentary would exclude page 4 and possibly incorporate pages 5 and 6 together. In a series a synopsis of at least one of the programmes is needed so that an indication of the structure of the film can be grasped — clearly this is essential for a one-off programme. Unless a clear plan of the programme is available it is very hard for a production manager to present practical and realistic solutions for the making of the programme. A draft budget is helpful as an

INDEX

PROPOSAL

PROPOSED SUBJECTS

TREATMENT

EXAMPLE PROGRAMME

DRAFT BUDGET

APPENDIX

THE DISMAL SCIENCE

A proposal for a series of programmes about economists and their theories.

L. Tooke,
F. Harrison,
R. Gates,
FAIRFAX FILMS,
40 YONGE PARK,
LONDON, N4 3NT.

Date

PROPOSAL

We propose to make a series of six programmes about economists and their economic theories. These programmes are aimed towards being educational as well as entertaining but are not intended to be deep studies of economic theory.

As Carlyle said, 'Economics is the dismal science'. Yet it is a subject which affects us all and therefore some understanding of the theorists their theories and how they arrived at their conclusions must be of some importance in our lives.

As well as looking at their ideas we propose to look at their lives to see how their theories were shaped by their own experience. In this way we hope to show that economics has a real meaning for the viewers' everyday lives.

We are proposing that each of these programmes be thirty (30) minutes in length and they be shot on videotape.

Date

PROPOSED SUBJECTS

ADAM SMITH - THE FIRST ECONOMIST
Laid the theoretical foundations of the free market. He would be gratified that the command economies now recognize the superior virtues of individual enterprise. But why has the 'invisible hand' left 30 million people without jobs in OECD countries today? Would he modify his model of the market?

DAVID RICARDO - THE LAW OF RENTS
His theory of rent filled the gap in Smith's framework and identified the source of unearned income: land. But today - surprisingly, in the face of all the evidence - economists play down the importance of rent and the role of land in production. How would Ricardo react?

THOMAS MALTHUS - THE DISMAL SCIENTIST
Although his insights were more sociological than economic, his theory of wages served to shape people's attitudes even to this day: economics evidently is the dismal science! Or is it? The evidence does not confirm a correlation between fertility and living standards/economic growth.

HENRY GEORGE - THE MAN WHO WOULD ABOLISH TAXES
Standing at the crossroads of the old and the new worlds, he was not as cautious as his predecessors or, indeed, his successors. His ideas, though popular at the time, were resisted. Was this by reason or prejudice?

KARL MARX - THE SOCIALIST ECONOMIST
The man behind the basic political division of the world, which evolved from his economic thinking. Some still say 'Better dead than red' but clearly this attitude is harder to maintain in the light of current political changes.

J.M. KEYNES - THE INFLATIONARY SOLUTION
Unemployment has always been an unpopular subject electorally and particularly so between the wars. Keynes' suggestion was to relieve the problem by expanding demand. This solution was seized upon by governments all over the world, but has his theory really provided the solution?

TREATMENT

All the programmes will follow the same structure and for the most part will be shot in a studio setting.

In each programme an actor, dressed and made up to look like the relevant economist, will be placed in a stylized study or library appropriate to the period of the particular subject. The set will incorporate a chroma-key screen, so that relevant visuals can be introduced to highlight the economist's words and theories. The economist will be interviewed by another actor playing the role of the programme's anchor-man.

Thus, on one level, the programme will be familiar to the modern audience.

The opening section of the programme will cover the life and times of the individual economist and will use the chroma-key to illustrate the history with drawings or photographs of the period.

Once the historical background of the economist has been covered the middle section of the programme will consider the key points of the character's economic thinking. Whenever opinions are given they will be quotes from the person's own writings. In the process of answering the interviewer's questions the economist's explanations will be illustrated by diagrams on the chroma-key screen and by this method we expect to explain, in a simplified form, some of the more complex theories.

The concluding section of the programme will revert to a modern disciple of the economist who will relate the original thinker's ideas to contemporary issues.

EXAMPLE PROGRAMME
HENRY GEORGE

The programme opens with the anchor-man giving a brief introduction which will include the comments that the man we are to meet has been described by Einstein as someone whose work is such that 'One cannot imagine a more beautiful combination of intellectual keenness, artistic form and fervent love of justice'. This man is the American economist Henry George.

The interviewer moves across to meet the actor playing George and opens the debate by commenting that George is known as the economist who would abolish taxes but before looking at his theories could he tell us a little of his life.

George states that he was born in Philadelphia in 1839 into a land that was rich in opportunities. By the time the settlers were hitting the edge of the western frontier he had arrived in San Francisco and had already been a seaman, newspaperman and general worker. It was through these experiences that his conscience as a social critic was developed and his passionate awareness of how the tax system inhibited workers from earning wages began to evolve.

This evolution led to his writing PROGRESS AND POVERTY which, in the beginning, was rejected by US publishers so that George had to hand set the first edition himself. The book became a bestseller.

At this point the anchor-man leads the discussion towards the theories themselves ... The debate between the interviewer and George looks at the influence that his work had on the tax policies in British politics, particularly the last major constitutional crisis of 1909.

With George's death, in 1897, the interviewer returns to the main set and introduces a contemporary American economist who supports George's theories.

The contemporary economist will comment on the actions proposed by Ronald Reagan's tax cutting gurus and he will look at the reasons why these policies failed to reach the statute book and will finally say why, as an advocate of George, he believes George's thinking should be followed today.

DRAFT BUDGET   THE DISMAL SCIENCE   Date

For six half-hour programmes shot in a studio on video tape.

A Story and Script   —
B Producers fee   — £
   Directors fee   — £
   Writers fee   — £

C Salaries; Production (pm.pa.re)   — £
              Crew   — £
              Editing   — £
              Additional   — £

D Art department   — £
E Artistes; Cast   — £
F Music; Direction, Musicians   — £
G Costumes and wigs   — £
H Misc. production stores   — £
I Video stock   Ratio @ 6 to 1   — £
J Laboratory charges   — £
   Studio   — £
   Editing Off line   — £
           On line   — £

K Equipment   — £
L Power   — £
M Travel & transport; Location   — £
                        Studio   — £

N Hotel & living exp; Location   — £
O Insurances   — £
P PAYE/SIC   — £
Q Publicity salaries & expenses   — £
R Miscellaneous expenses   — £
S Sets & models; construction   — £
                  props/dressing   — £
U Location facilities   — £

Y Finance & legal   — £
Z Overheads   — £

TOTAL   £

PAGE 7

APPENDIX

ADDITIONAL INFORMATION

LETTERS OF SUPPORT

PAGE 8

indication of the likely cost and this too can only be realized from the treatment, and the appendix should be used to provide evidence that the programme can be made.

Whatever project is planned the script (for a feature), the proposal (for a documentary), the storyboard and copy (for a commercial), or any combination of these forms of presentation are the first steps to get the money to make the film.

Once the money is obtained the pre-production proper can begin.

CHAPTER 5

PRE-PRODUCTION

A picture is made a success not on a set but over the drawing board.
Cecil B. De Mille.

With the finance in place the pre-production period of a film now begins.

This is the time when the mechanics of the production are put together and the materials and the team who are to realize the film are gathered. In building terms it is the time when the blueprint of the script is translated into the solid forms of work schedules, materials and labour and the detailed working drawings or, in other words, the shooting script and possibly the storyboard, are drawn up. Obviously the more precise the blueprint, or the more detailed the shooting script, the better the opportunity for making the right decisions.

This also is a time when the alternatives and options can be explored by the key creative personnel. It is cheaper for the director and the camera person to visit a location, discuss the likely shots, and revise the shooting script and plans accordingly, than to have a crew standing around while these decisions are made. A feature crew on a low-budget film of, say, about £2 million, costs about £800–£1000 an hour in wages alone and on top of this there is equipment hire time and actors' fees. It is therefore a costly business and consequently bad management to have long discussions about how to shoot a particular scene and to leave the crew and cast standing around waiting for instructions.

Therefore we are back to the prime role of the production manager which is management: the management of resources, that is money, labour, time, of which the most important is time. It is the use of time and knowing what needs to be done and what can be left for the moment that has to be appreciated by the production manager and the production office.

A basic scheme for organizing a film in the pre-production period is outlined in Figure 5.1. This is an indication of the order in which various parts of a production may be considered and who is responsible for each area. It should be noted that the producer is in reality responsible for the whole but as the production progresses the producer will delegate some duties and retain others. To what extent this delegation takes place depends on the individual producer and can be almost none, at

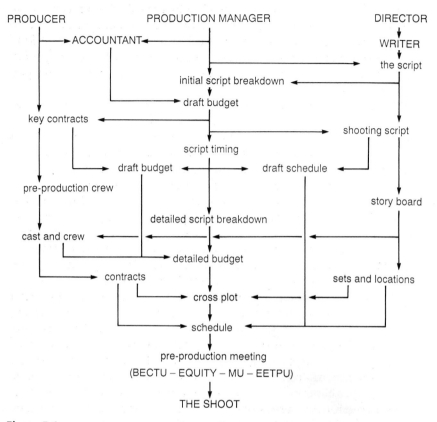

Figure 5.1

one end of the scale, to almost total, at the other end. An example of the latter concerned a British production manager who was given the total package by an American producer and told that the producer expected to see a first assembly of the proposed film in 4 months' times after which the American producer returned to the United States. This is a rare exception but it does show that there are no golden rules in the business of production and production management.

With this example in mind the first point to consider is who are the prime movers on a production and what their relationship is. The key people are the producer, production manager, director and writer. The producer may well have hired in the other three or there may be some other relationship between these people, for example it is not uncommon to have producer/directors and writer/directors and on occasion producer/director/writers. The producer/director is quite a usual role on a documentary but there comes a time on every production when one person cannot perform more than one key role and therefore a production manager should be hired to run the production so that the producer/director can fulfil his or her roles as the director.

The one other person who will need to be consulted at an early stage is an accountant. The producer and/or production manager on a documentary film should be well able to deal with the budget for that kind of production but the size of budget on a feature will require professional advice and this should be sought at the beginning of the pre-production phase.

With the key people in place the next stage is taken: the script – as has been said before, no script (or idea), no film.

Once the script has been accepted a budget has to be calculated. A draft budget can best be estimated from a breakdown of the script. This job may be done by the producer in the first instance, but is a production management task. The producer's breakdown will only be an indication because a good production manager will want to be involved as it will help to indicate the problems and demands that will come up during the production. Of course, a draft budget may have been prepared during the development period of the production and therefore at this stage the production manager should be looking at this draft to see how it matches up with the way the film is proceeding.

While the draft budget is being produced, or checked, the producer will be trying to place key contracts. Key contracts are for major actors, key crew, and any other personnel who may be essential for the production. On documentaries this will include essential interviewees; on a feature the stars will probably be part of the development package as will the director and script writer, so their contracts will already be in place although there will be a number of other people who are essential for the successful conclusion of the film. These may include, for example, Oscar-winning lighting directors, art directors, composers and other specialists.

Once the production has reached this stage the director, and possibly the writer, in conjunction with the production manager, should be working on the shooting script. With a complete shooting script the production manager can begin work on a more accurate budget and a draft schedule, but in order to do this properly an idea of the time length of the script is needed and therefore a timing has to be estimated.

The usual way of estimating the likely length of a drama script is to assume a page to be equal to a minute of screen time, but only a detailed inspection of the script will show how true this estimate may be. The surest way of script timing is for the director, or failing them, the script supervisor to act out each scene against a stop watch. If the director can do it, so much the better, as they will have more of a sense of how long the dramatic pauses should be and how long any action shots, passing cars, charging horses etc., should be held. For example, it has been known for a script to have the simple wording 'Scene XX. There is a battle' and clearly a battle, depending on its complexity, can take up a considerable amount of screen time. Therefore the estimation of the eventual length of the film is an important stage in the production process and may be one of the points where compromise in a production begins. Although the eventual length of a feature film may not need to fit a precise time, a film made for television usually has to fit a specific slot, which will have a time limit on it, and therefore it is vital to ensure that the script or proposal can be made within the constraints of the contract.

The money for a production will only buy so much time and if the early estimates are in line with the director's aims then the schedule and budget will match. On the other hand, if the director wants vast crowds or exotic locations or luxurious sets or amazing effects and stunts or, possibly worse still, all of these, then something has to give or the producer has to find the extra money, assuming it is not already in place. This is why the next stage, the budget and the schedule, has to be looked at in great detail and with much care.

The production of the budget and the schedule will take some time because they have an effect on each other; in simple terms a longer shoot means more money and if more money is not available then the shoot has to be shortened. This is true of any part of a production but the shooting period is usually the most costly in terms of time and therefore the area to look at first if money has to be saved. Potentially one of the great time savers, and consequently money savers, in modern production is the computer provided it is used properly. A production manager would be strongly advised to consider the use of the budgeting and scheduling packages that are available from companies like d.Sam Limited for desktop computers. Because the detailed business of budgeting and scheduling is an exercise of 'what if?', the aim being to find out 'what' happens 'if' a particular policy is pursued, a computer can do the arithmetic for this kind of exercise far more quickly and efficiently than even the most experienced production manager or production accountant.

While the budget and schedule are being worked out the producer and director should be proceeding with their next steps which are the appointment of the pre-production crew and, when it is used, the drawing up of a storyboard.

The pre-production crew will include the production office, the art department, construction crew, location finders, researchers and any other people who may be needed to get the production on the road. They are usually employed after a discussion between the producer and the production manager. The director and the art department may begin to prepare a storyboard at this time. This essentially is a visual interpretation of the script and some directors, like Steven Spielberg or the late Alfred Hitchcock, like very detailed storyboards while others are happy with key shots. In the commercials' film world storyboards are invariably drawn as they usually are part of the advertising agency's presentation.

The one time a storyboard is essential is for special effects sequences. When films like *2001*, *Those Magnificent Men in Their Flying Machines* and *Star Wars* have shots or sequences in them which require the compilation of two, three or more overlays of different film, then the technicians need a precise idea of what will be wanted and a storyboard drawing is the best way of presenting a concept of the final visual.

During this period the production manager should be finalizing the detailed breakdown of the script. The breakdown should be started as soon as the shooting script is available. It is the skeleton from which the budget, cross-plot and schedule are developed, and these have to be in place before detailed costing and other activities can begin.

With the pre-production crew in place and the shooting script to hand the business of pulling the screenplay to pieces begins, so that it can be organized into the components that are needed for the production of a cross-plot and a shooting schedule. While this action is followed the producer and the production manager should be finalizing contracts with the shooting crew, post-production personnel and any other technicians or cast yet to be employed. When all this information is in place a detailed budget, if not already completed, can be calculated or refined.

While the production office is finalizing the contracts and budget the art department should be progressing towards set construction, if it is required, and the location manager towards confirming locations where these are required.

The drawing up of a cross-plot should take place at this stage (the purpose of a cross-plot will be explained in Chapter 7). With the aid of the cross-plot the last parts of pre-production can be put into place and a detailed schedule drawn up.

This leaves one final action that has to be taken before shooting can begin on a feature film: the pre-production meeting with the unions. This meeting, which is designed to confirm to both the producer and the unions that there will be no upset on the production, is not required for low-budget productions like documentaries, pop-promos or commercials.

It should be realized that Figure 5.1 shows a simplified scheme for the steps to be taken by a production manager in the pre-production phase of a film or programme.

A documentary will not usually require a storyboard, casting, art direction, set construction or cross-plot. On the other hand, a very-large-budget feature will have a much more complicated pattern particularly because the exercise of defining and refining the budget and schedule, both of which influence each other, may continue over a much longer period than is indicated in the above scheme.

To understand the reasons for some of this complexity it is necessary to look at the individual parts of the pre-production process.

CHAPTER 6

SCRIPT BREAKDOWN

Before a shoot can begin two main questions need to be answered. These are: how long will it take to produce the film and how much will the production cost? Or, in other words, what is the schedule and the budget? As has already been stated these two factors are inter-related and any change in one will have an effect on the other.

Therefore one of the first problem the producer or production manager has to solve is how to arrive at an estimate of the time needed to complete the production because, in turn, this information will provide part of the solution for the costing of the production. The best way to arrive at a more precise estimate for the likely length of the film is to do a breakdown of the script or shooting script, if it is ready.

A script breakdown essentially is the business of splitting the script into its individual parts, or sequences, and analysing each part to see what is required in terms of the production.

Now a shot may be very simple or highly complex and clearly the more complex the shot the longer it is going to take to film. At its most simple all that is required is for a camera to be set up and turned on for a desired length of time with no movement, no extra lighting, no performance and possibly no sound. The crew required for this kind of shot can be the bare minimum and therefore the most economic. Probably the most common example of this kind of shot, with the possible exception of the constraint on lighting, is the 'pack shot' in a commercial or the 'scenic' shot, which occurs in every form of production.

At its most complex a shot can be very spectacular and involve extensive camera movement, including tracking, panning, tilting and craning action, large cast and various special effects. The most obvious examples of this sort of shot can be seen in battle sequences in films like *Waterloo* and *War and Peace* or in the set dance sequences in musical films like *West Side Story* and *Hello Dolly*, where the choreographer's art may take over from the stunt co-ordinator's skills in providing the spectacular; although it should be remembered that the director is still in overall charge. Thus it can be concluded that the only limits to the complexity of a shot are the director's imagination and/or the size of the budget.

46

The first step in the process of breaking the script down is to do an initial analysis of the number of scenes in the script and this can most easily be done by compiling a list of all the sets and locations, containing the scenes to be shot in each, with details of the requirements for each scene. Figure 6.1 shows this initial breakdown applied to the example script, 'Wizard'.

The next step in the process of breaking the script down is to count the likely number of shots in the eventual film and, if there is a shooting script available, the simple answer to this question is to see what the final shot number is. The number of shots then have to be evaluated in terms of the number of 'set-ups' in the production as it is the 'set-ups' which will have the main influence on the time taken to film each scene and consequently the overall time taken to shoot the production.

A 'set-up' is the business of setting up the camera in order to take one or more shots. Thus in filming a conversation between two characters the director may have decided on three 'set-ups', a close up on character A, a close up on character B and a two-shot on both characters. The shooting script may show that the sequence begins with the two-shot then cuts to a close up on A followed by a close up on B, then back to A, then to B, another two-shot, back to B, then A and ending with a two-shot. So, in the planned final film, we have nine cuts but only three 'set-ups'. In the example script in Chapter 3 (Figures 3.2 and 3.5) the tracking shot 6.3 (page v) would almost certainly be started at 6.1 and be continued through 6.3, 6.5 and on to 6.7. The close-up shot 6.2 would probably be done as one 'set-up', the close-up shot 6.4 being a separate 'set-up'. It should be remembered that the editor may yet change this plan when the final cut is assembled but the plan is still needed if the right production decisions are to be made.

From the various shots in the shooting script the production manager needs to group similar ones together and thereby arrive at a list of 'set-ups'. These shots can come from any part of the shooting script as the only factor under consideration at this stage is the similarity of each 'set-up'.

It should be remembered that the business of lighting, re-lighting, laying tracks, and generally preparing for a shot can take a lot of time and that sometimes it may be quicker to re-dress the set or for the cast to change costume than it is to set up a new shot. It is this management of time and the correct evaluation of the time resource which provides the challenge to a production manager.

A 90 minute shooting script may have anything from 300 to 1000 shots in it depending on the director's style of working and the sort of film it is, although there are always exceptions.

Once these shots have been organized into 'set-ups', each 'set-up' has to be considered for the work involved in achieving each shot. This aspect of production management is almost impossible to define in terms of how much time any particular shot may require because each shot is individual. However, the broad guidelines, indicated above, that have to be considered by the production manager can be listed as follows.

SET: Int. CHRIS'S OFFICE

Location: Shepperton Studio.   Sheet No. 5

Set requirements: Practical telephone. Light box.

SCENE NOS	D/N	PAGES	CHARACTERS	CROWD	PROPS	SYNOPSIS & NOTES
9	D	$4^3/_4$	MELANIE CHRIS RICHARD JENNY ANDREW	None	Box Globe	Conversation about box TRACKING SHOTS REQUIRED
13	D	$3^1/_4$	CHRIS MELANIE RICHARD JENNY ANDREW	None	Contracts Working phone Coffee	Discussion on security
16	D	4	CHRIS MELANIE RICHARD ANDREW PROFESSOR SPIELBERG JENNY	Lab. technician Security officer	None	The travel offer TRACKING SHOTS REQUIRED

Figure 6.1

The location or set

The point to be considered when looking at this factor is how much control there is over the shooting location and what the likely effect is on the time taken to set up. A studio set is under the production's complete control but a location can have interference from all kinds of sources, the weather, people watching, extraneous noises from vehicles or aircraft as well as a hundred and one other irritations which cannot be guessed at during the pre-production stage of the film. The only solution is to give the production more time when planning a location shoot.

The cast

How many are involved in the shot? Clearly the larger the number the longer it takes to organize the shot and if crowds are used then other factors have to be taken into consideration, like how many additional production crew, in the form of assistant directors, are needed to direct them in addition to the extended catering, travel and other logistical requirements.

Crowds can be difficult to manage simply because of the effort needed to maintain their concentration. During the filming of *Grand Prix* there was a scene where a flaming car is driven into the pits. It was about 4 o'clock in the afternoon and the director, John Frankenheimer, was disgusted by the crowd's lack of reaction to the dramatic action during the rehearsals. They appeared to be more interested in their tea break. Frankenheimer called his special effects man over and told him to 'blow up the tea van' when given the signal. The unit went for a take. The flaming sports car came into the pits. The crowd looked on. The signal was given and the tea truck exploded. The crowd reacted and Frankenheimer got his shot! This is an extreme example of how to direct crowds but it also shows that a production manager can only guess at the factors which may eventually be employed in completing a shot.

Camera movement

It should be obvious that the more complicated the camera movement the more time is needed to rehearse in order to be sure that the right answer is obtained on film. Also there will be times when a scene demands the use of two or more cameras. In features this is usually for battle scenes, chases, crashes and other spectacular visuals, whereas on documentaries multi-camera set-ups are used for covering pop concerts or other momentous events. The cameras themselves may be static but the organization of each crew so that they all know what is expected of them can be even more time consuming than any complicated single-camera set-up.

The classic film shaggy dog story concerns the problems of multiple camera set-ups. During the filming of Cecil B. De Mille's *The Ten Commandments* there was a sequence where the Israelites were fleeing Egypt. It was late in the afternoon and the light was fading. The cameras rolled and the action began. On completion of the shot De Mille turned to his first unit, only to be told that it was no good; the second unit also had a camera problem; the third unit in the crowd had had its lens obscured; and the fourth unit had been knocked by a camel. The only hope for some footage rested with the fifth unit doing a long hot. De Mille rang them and asked how was it for them? The reply came 'Ready when you are C.B.'

Other special requirements

These can include technical requirements for sound, lighting or special effects or the use of any specialist equipment. This latter category should include stunts, choreography or any other specialist discipline which requires a particular understanding, for example the peculiar problems presented by trainers with their animal performers.

It will be seen from the short list above that each production has to be considered on its merits and each shot on its individual needs, and a step in this process is to list who and what exceptional items are needed for each scene, that is lists of the cast and crew, equipment, location details, props, notes on special effects, in fact information on any and every aspect covering the production of each shot. What is being looked for is any item in the script which may affect the time taken to complete the shot.

Thus, taking the example script in Chapter 3 which is the first 5 minutes or so of screen time for a feature film, a breakdown would produce the following information.

There are 41 cuts in the five scenes described and these amount to 28 'set-ups'.

Four of the scenes are outside and one is an interior. The interior opens the option for filming on a location or in a studio. This is a decision which depends on a number of varying factors but in this instance will probably be on a location because it is likely to be easier and cheaper to find a suitable office than to build a set.

Sets will be required for later scenes in the film but with modern cameras, tape recorders and film techniques the constraints which used to demand the building of sets are long gone. However, this does not mean that there are no benefits from working in a studio. As ever, it will be a case of evaluating the needs of the particular production. In any case, there may well be a degree of set construction in order to create the site of the dig and the sheep pen in the clump of trees, but this will depend on the final location.

Of the cast presented so far two, Richard and Melanie, are key players, one, Chris, has a character role and the other three are bit players although all will be appearing in later scenes. At this stage in the script there are no crowd scenes or other casting problems which might require additional assistant directors or other facilities beyond the usual needs of a feature unit.

In respect of the demands of the camera none of the shots require anything more complicated than tracking, so basic equipment should be all that is needed. All the shots are in daylight, so overtime or unsocial hours payments for the crew should not need to be considered during this period of the shoot.

One of the special requirements that will have to be kept in kind for the exteriors is the weather, particularly as a showery day is described in the script, and time will have to be built into the schedule to allow for the opportunity to be taken to get the right kind of weather. A showery day can be solved by having special effects rain available but generally 'weather cover' has to be allowed for in every production, even those that are inside. During the filming of Clive Donner's production of *The Caretaker* it snowed outside. Knowing that snow in England does not usually last and not wishing to break continuity by having the exterior snow covered in one shot and plain in the next, the cameras were pointed away from the windows to begin with. The snow lasted throughout the shoot with the results that there are few scenes showing the outside.

Depending on the designer, there may be special requirements for costume and vehicle styles. The other props which have to be provided are the globe, the lead box and a plan of the site, this last item being bold enough to be seen on screen.

The title sequence also falls into this part of the breakdown but it will be dealt with separately, after the principal photography has been completed. However, it must be borne in mind that the opening shot is part of the titles and therefore will have to be treated differently, probably by shooting more footage than might initially be thought to be required by the script.

It should now be clear why no real progress on a production can begin until the shooting script has been produced.

The breakdown on a documentary should follow the same pattern. Again the purpose is to analyse the demands of the production to see what is required.

Visiting the locations with the director and the camera person or director of photography can be one of the major ways of saving time in the long run and clarifying what will be wanted at each place and for each 'set-up'.

All the information gathered should be listed appropriately and it should be realized that all this information will be needed to prepare not only the shooting schedule but also the daily call sheets, movement orders and other necessary instructions and information for the successful realization of the film.

```
                        SCENE BREAKDOWN


Production: WIZARD
SCENE: 9                    PAGE: 4³⁄₄
TIME: Day              INT/EXT:Interior SCHEDULE DATE: Thursday 26th..
SEASON: Unknown          WEATHER: None
SET: Chris Watson's office
LOCATION:   South West Technical College,
              (address)
MAIN CHARACTERS:   Chris Watson         MINOR CHARACTERS: Andrew
                   Richard Fairfax                        Jenny
                   Melanie Fairfax
ACTION PROPS:   Metal box        EXTRAS: None
                Crystal globe
SPECIAL EFFECTS: None   EQUIPMENT: Tracks
```

Figure 6.2

```
                      LOCATION BREAKDOWN


Production: WIZARD
LOCATION: South West Technical College
MAP REFERENCE: A to Z page, reference
ADDRESS: South West Technical College
        Address and phone no.
CONTACT: Contact name              ON SITE PROD. OFFICE
        Address and phone no.    Address and phone no.
OTHER CONTACTS: Police + address and phone no.
                Hospital with casualty + address and phone no.
                (Equipment supply + address and phone no.)
                (Other contacts + address and phone no.)
SETS: Chris Watson's office
      Classroom
      Corridor
      Animal (Guardian's) office
      Weapons office
      Preparation room
COMMENTS: The shooting period is during the college's Easter break
          and crew will only have limited access. Please do not
          interfere with any material that is in place. Any
          queries or problems can be referred through the site
          production office.
DIRECTION: From the production office. Take the...
```

Figure 6.3

One of the forms that this tabulation may take is the listing of the requirements for each individual scene, which would produce a document looking something like Figure 6.2.

Another way of tabulating the script information is by each individual place and this produces the location document, Figure 6.3.

The location breakdown will not be able to be completed until all the possible locations have been visited and therefore the production office is in the usual 'chicken or egg' situation. A lot of the necessary information has to be given at a time when there is no possibility of completing it but this in turn helps define what may be wanted eventually.

There is a third list relevant to the breakdown of the script which should be prepared and this is a schedule of the cast involved because, like the scenes and locations, the cast is another factor which varies from day to day during the shoot and all these variables need to be accounted for. One way to present this information is shown in Figure 6.4.

```
                       CAST  BREAKDOWN
    _____

    Production: WIZARD
    PRODUCTION ADDRESS: Address and phone no.
    PERSONNEL RECORD: Name of Actor
    JOB: Actor
    PART: Merlyn
    ADDRESS: Address and phone no.  AGENT:  Name
                                            Address and phone
                                            no.
    CAST: Days worked - 0
    NAT. INS. NO.: YS 09 98 95 C
    PAID ON SALARY.
    CONTRACT TYPE: Separated periods
    PAY RATES: Daily rate          £    50.00
               Exploitation rate % £   125.00
               Other % rate        £    75.00
               Overtime (daily)    £    16.67
               Overtime (weekly)   £    10.00
    TOTAL COST:                    £  6300.00
    APPEARING IN SCENES:
          3 22 23 24 27 28 29 30 33 34 35 36 37 39 40 41
          45 46 etc...(to final scenes)...135 136
    LOCATIONS:
    The standing room    Forest clearing    The Birks of A.
    Bray                 Devon Road         etc...
    SETS:
    The fortress         The great hall     The dungeon
    Time machine         Merlyn's home      Kitchen
    Uther's chamber      etc...
```

Figure 6.4

It will be noted that part of the information included on this cast breakdown is the contract cost for the artiste, which is relevant to the eventual budget of the production. The way this cost is made up will depend on the contractual arrangements agreed with the artiste or their agent but it needs to be remembered, when considering this item, that the production is buying more than the artiste's immediate performance. On commercials the artiste usually gets a fee for every time the film is broadcast and this is possible because of the short life span of a commercial. Because a feature may have a much longer life it is usual to buy the rights to exploit the artiste's performance for all the ways the film may eventually be used, including video, broadcast, satellite, etc. Hence the exploitation fee for which the precise terms will depend on the contract.

The information relating to which scenes, locations and sets the performer is appearing in will be of use to the artiste in question but is of more importance for the production office as another way to confirm that the performer, who is a variable item, has not been overlooked in the scheduling. Similar lists should be drawn up for action props, that is to say props which are directly involved in the action of a scene. In the example script above this would cover the crystal globe and the lead box.

The preparation of these schedules may seem to be a lot of work for little apparent return but the long-term use for this information is in the preparation of the daily call sheets and movement orders and the immediate use for these tabulated pages is in the construction of a cross-plot. The real return for this work is usually only seen in the negative since when a vital prop or person is not available on set when wanted, with the result that a unit is left standing unable to work but being paid for even as it stands. These are the moments when bad pre-production shows and good pre-production pays off.

CHAPTER 7

THE CROSS-PLOT

Having broken down the script and organized the information acquired into particular categories the next thing to be done with the material is to use it.

As said already, one of the purposes of this information is the production of a schedule, and one of the tools in achieving this end is the cross-plot.

Essentially a cross-plot is a way of organizing the different scenes in a production against what is required in each of these individual scenes, but firstly the information needed for this has to be collated.

The first step in the collation is to produce a schedule of the scenes in order, and this document should look something like Figure 7.1.

The first list is tabulated in scene order. The next two letters denote (e) exterior or (i) interior and (d) day or (n) night. Some production managers also note the Script Day/Time at this point as it can help define the shot which is being looked for and therefore the time it should be scheduled. The scene heading or LOCATION comes next with the MAIN CHARACTER, MINOR CHARACTER, SPECIAL EFFECTS and ACTION PROPS following. SPECIAL EFFECTS covers items like gun shots, bullet wounds, blood, explosions, fog, wind machines, rain and any other effect that is photographed at the time of filming. This heading excludes those special effects, like the firing of laser guns in *Star Wars*, which are processed into the film by the laboratories at a later stage. ACTION PROPS covers any item used by the performers during the scene; this ranges from cars to food, suitcases, papers, televisions, musical instruments, model bats (for Dracula films), and, in the case of the example script, a lead box, a crystal globe and the site plans for the archaeological dig.

This schedule now has to be reorganized into set and location order by grouping each location together. From the reorganization shown in Figure 7.2, it will be seen that not only do scenes 2 and 6, and 9, 13 and 16 come together, but there are some scenes from later in the script which are at the same locations and consequently are placed with their relevant scenes. So scene 107 follows scene 1 and 108 is placed between scenes 6 and 3, this latter placing is done because scene 108 is similar to scene 6 and consequently is more likely to result in the same or similar set-up. It should be noted that these schedules are working documents

LOCATION	MAIN CHARACTER	MINOR CHARACTER	SPECIAL EFFECTS	ACTION PROPS
1 e d North Devon	Richard Melanie	—	—	Richard's car
2 e d Site of dig	Richard Melanie	Jenny David	—	Richard's car
3 e d Under bridge near site	Melanie	—	—	Teddy bear Book Mirror Lipstick
4 e d Fields near site	Melanie Merlyn	—	—	Crystal globe
5 e d Tree-covered hill near site	Melanie Merlyn	—	—	Crystal globe Lead box Nail file
6 e d Site of dig	Richard Melanie	Jenny David 2 Archaeologists	—	Site plans Lead box
7 e d Entrance of Greenham History Research Institute	Richard Melanie	Jenny 2 Guards	—	Richard's car
8 i d Security office	Richard Melanie Chris	Jenny 3 Security Guards	—	Melanie's bag

etc.

LOCATION	MAIN CHARACTER	MINOR CHARACTER	SPECIAL EFFECTS	ACTION PROPS
1 e d North Devon	Richard Melanie	–	–	Richard's car
107 e d North Devon	Richard Melanie	–	–	Richard's car
2 e d Site of dig	Richard Melanie	Jenny David	–	Richard's car
6 e d Site of dig	Richard Melanie	Jenny David	–	Site plans Lead box
108 e d Site of dig	Richard Melanie	2 Archaeologists Georgia Archaeologist	–	–
3 e d Under bridge near site	Melanie	–	–	Teddy bear Book Mirror Lipstick Crystal globe
4 e d Fields near site	Melanie Merlyn	–	–	Crystal globe
5 e d Tree-covered hill near site	Melanie Merlyn	–	–	Crystal globe Lead box Nail file
7 e d Entrance of Greenham History Research Institute	Richard Melanie	Jenny Guard	–	Richard's car
8 i d Security office	Richard Melanie Chris	Jenny Security Guard	–	Melanie's bag
9 i d Chris's office	Melanie Richard Chris	Andrew Jenny	–	Lead box
13 i d Chris's office	Richard Melanie Chris	Andrew Professor S.	–	Phone
16 i d Chris's office	Chris Melanie Richard	Jenny Andrew Professor S. Jenny Technician Security Officer	–	Phone

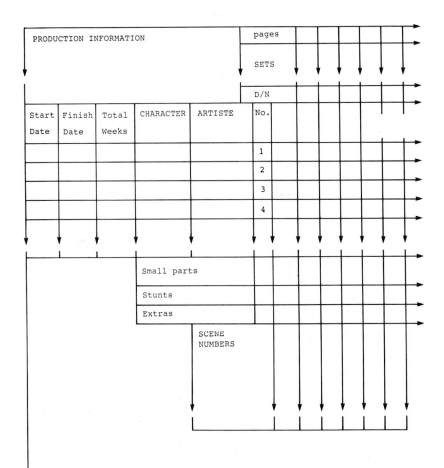

Figure 7.3

and are not intended to be seen by people outside the production office. Therefore they do not need to have the identifying titling which call sheets and similar documents will have. Understanding this basic principle of re-organizing the breakdown information, many production managers arrive at the same solution by simply shuffling their breakdown sheets into a shooting order. This eliminates the need for separate lists.

It should be remembered that the only time a production is being productive is when film is going through the camera. This is the whole purpose of the business and time spent on other activities, like travel, setting up, rehearsal and striking, although not wasted, is certainly not productive in this sense.

Consequently the simple logic is to shoot as much of any individual set-up on any one location at one time, as is compatible with the requirements of the script; this latter fact is important because a screen-

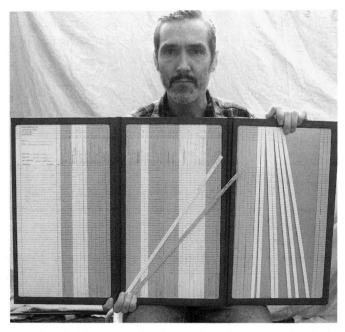

Figure 7.4 Author holding a strip/production board. One strip has been removed. Different colours denote different situations.

play may demand certain weather conditions and consequently two or more different schedules may well have to be drawn up to accommodate the different weather needs. During the shooting of David Lean's film *Ryan's Daughter* the schedule was drawn up on the basis of the weather available. Each day the decision on which scenes were to be shot depended on the type of clouds in view. Therefore short-term schedules were needed so the choices could be made; it also made the film the most expensive of its day.

This reorganized list will provide the basis for a draft schedule and cross-plot. The cross-plot is a scheme from which the final schedule can be prepared. Essentially, the body of a blank CROSS-PLOT will look something like Figure 7.3.

Thus on one axis against the shooting dates, information about each scene is noted: the scene number, location or set, day or night shoot and number of pages of script covered. On the other axis is listed the cast involved and any other details or information that may be relevant.

Most of the information in this blank should be self-explanatory but some points may not be immediately apparent. The first is the word 'pages' at the top of the sheet; this refers to the number of pages of script covered by the plot. The second is 'D/N', which simply defines if the scene is in Day or Night. The third is the 'No.' following the artiste; this is the number given to each character and, in a very long or detailed cross-plot, is a way of seeing which performer is being referred to without having to trace back to the source. The final point is the columns of scene numbers which are under their sets or locations; these numbers are

Production Co. FAIRFAX FILMS Ltd.	pages	3	2	2	12	4
Production WIZARD		field/stone	devon road	site	chris's office	lab/c dor
Producer *Name*						
Director *Name*	SETS					
Camera *Name*						
Art Director *Name*						
Editor *Name*						
	D/N	D	D	D	D	D

Start Date	Finish Date	Total Weeks	CHARACTER	ARTISTE	No.	TOTAL DAYS	23 / 4	24	25 / 4	26 / 4	27 / 4
24/4	9/7	7	Richard	*Name*	1	32		1	1	1	1
23/4	17/7	8	Melanie	*Name*	2	37	2	2	2	2	2
23/4	1/7	6	Merlyn	*Name*	3	23	3				
26/4	3/5	1	Chris	*Name*	4	5				4	4
26/4	3/5	1	Andrew	*Name*	5	5				5	5
25/4	25/4	1	Jenny	*Name*	6	1			6		
25/4	25/4	1	David	*Name*	7	1			7		
			Small parts		A				a		
			Stunts		B						
			Extras		C						
			SCENE NUMBERS				3 34	1 107	2 108 4	5 8 12 18	6 7

Figure 7.5a

derived from the shooting script and, besides indicating how much has to be done on any one set or location, can be used to check that the work has been done by crossing each number off as the scene is completed.

The details of the shoot are now put into this format. It should be noted that it does not matter on which axis the information is placed although the usual and most common form is with the cast on the vertical axis and the dates on the horizontal. The standard cross-plot form and the American strip boards are all printed on this basis.

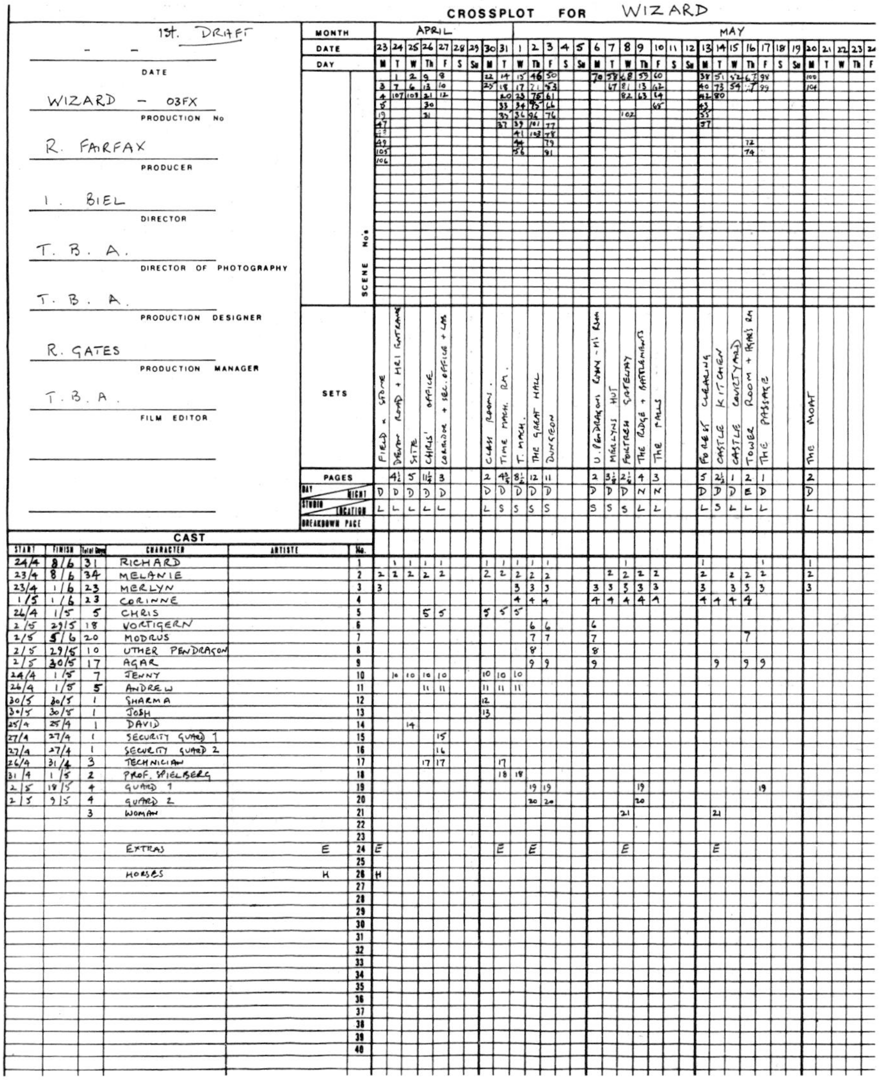

Figure 7.5b

Obviously a production with only three or four characters and a lot of scenes will result in a plot which has an oblong shape, and this may be more conveniently organized in a north–south configuration rather than the conventional east–west configuration, but the eventual decision should depend on the needs of the individual production.

In the first instance the placing of the information is done by taking the sets in the order provided by the revised location schedule and noting which characters appear in these particular scenes and, where the character and scene meet, this is noted on the plot by the character's number being written in the appropriate square. The result is that a pattern appears on the plot indicating when the characters are used and the frequency of their use.

So, using the location schedule in Figure 7.2, the first draft of the cross-plot will look like Figure 7.5a.

This then is the first draft of the cross-plot and, like all aspects of the pre-production period, it will undergo revisions depending on the need for it to meet various requirements. Indeed the first point to catch the eye is the '3' in the character Merlyn's plot. Is this the best use of this actor's time? Because the example script only covers the first few pages it cannot be known what other demands are being made on this character. However, the plot shows that the performer is required for 6 weeks, the first of which only has 1 day's work in it and the other 5 of which will involve 22 day's work. Therefore there is some spare time in the following weeks and it might be more economic to have the actor for 5 weeks and try to reschedule the first day's shoot.

The ideal, therefore, is to arrange the production so that each scene and its character are involved on a continuous basis with the result that, once the performers are no longer required or have completed their roles, they can be struck or released from the production. The more quickly a scene or character is used the more economically the production can be run. However, this is not always possible.

During the shooting of *Superman* the actor Marlon Brando was paid a reported fee of $1 million and, as well as this fee, his contract will certainly have specified his availability; consequently his character will have determined when his scene appeared in the cross-plot and in turn this will have decided which characters were also to appear on the same day. Furthermore, if any of those characters had to appear in any other scenes some effort will have been made to place all these scenes together. Clearly this is not always possible and it is the business of the production manager to evaluate the situation and hopefully come to the best compromise. If, for example, a minor character appears in the same scene as two of the picture's stars but one star is only available for the start of the shoot and the other is contracted to be on set at the end of the shoot, then the cross-plot will show a long gap between the call times for the minor character. All the production manager can do under these circumstances is to employ the actor playing the minor role for the duration of the whole shoot. This may seem expensive but it is necessary, for uncontracted actors are not obliged to refuse on the expectation that they will be called back to a production and stars who can command million-dollar fees do not expect to be told to change their schedules by a production manager.

The other option open to a production manager is a split contract. If there is a period of more than 5 weeks between the times the production requires the services of an artiste or technician, then a split contract may be offered. The usual form is for the contracted person to be paid a day's salary for every week between the contracted periods and this allows the artiste or technician to accept work on other productions which do not clash with the contracted periods of the split contract. An example of when this kind of contract was used is the filmed television series *A Piece of Cake* which required some winter scenes. The result was a split contract to cover a week's shoot in February followed by the rest of the shoot from May onwards. Television is the most likely occasion for the use of a split contract but clearly it is an option which has to be kept in mind when using actors on any long shoot.

Another point to remember is that key performers are often contracted for the entire film and therefore it matters not if they are apparently being used uneconomically in terms of time. Thus the actor playing Merlyn may well be being paid an 'above line' fee and his contract will specify his availability throughout the production. The producer will aim to have the actor available to the production for the period of the shoot, so, during the 8 weeks of the shoot, it will not make any real difference to the costings to the production as to when his 23 days of work occur.

One of the methods used by some production managers to help in the organization of the cross-plot is the strip board or production board. This is a piece of equipment, in the form of a board, which is laid out like a cross-plot but which allows the vertical columns denoting the scenes to be moved. This means that once the basic information is on each column the whole can be shuffled backwards and forwards until the user decides that the optimum order has been achieved. In other words the minimum time possible is spent in changing locations, the cast is hired for the shortest time and any other relevant items are only asked for as needed.

It should be realized that the production of the cross-plot is closely linked with the production of the schedule because it is from the cross-plot that the schedule is produced. The more complex the production the more detail is required in the cross-plot and the schedule. Thus with a documentary there may be no need for a cross-plot at all. However, as more and more factors come into play on a film then the greater the need for the cross-plot, particularly as it is the only way of seeing the shape of the whole production and consequently where time can best be saved.

It is a mistaken idea that the analysis of a script for production purposes, to produce a cross-plot, is a waste of time. It may well be time consuming to prepare but, in terms of cost, an hour saved during the shoot is often more money saved than the weekly salary of a production manager.

Time saved on the shoot is money saved on the production, which is why it is so important to get the schedule right.

CHAPTER 8

SCHEDULING FOR FEATURES

Time is money.

Proverb

Having got the information needed from the script by way of the script breakdown and cross-plot a schedule can be prepared. The schedule is the document which details what happens on which days of the shoot.

Everyone on the production should get a copy as it gives the basic outline of the work to be done. The reason for giving this information to all the crew is so they will know what they have to do each day and therefore can prepare themselves effectively. The detailed information for any particular day's work will be provided on the daily call sheet which must be issued at the latest on the day before, before the end of the working day. As a general rule, a production manager can never provide too much information and it is far better for the crew and cast to be skipping through detail they feel they do not need rather than asking for information they should have been provided with. It should be remembered that crews and particularly freelance technicians may well have met for the first time at the beginning of the production and as such they probably will not have established the sort of working relationship that occurs in industries where staff are permanently employed. Therefore any action or information which helps them work together more effectively should not be overlooked; indeed, it must be encouraged.

It is well known that films are not shot in script order but sometimes it is not realized how important it is to achieve the best possible order for the shoot by means of a properly worked-out schedule. These days this optimum order can sometimes be achieved more quickly and easily with the aid of computer programs. These programs are available from specialist software companies which, like all the businesses which service the film industry, are noted in one or other of the trade directories. The real advantage of the scheduling programs is that they let the user play 'what if?' with a schedule and very quickly show the consequences of different options when applied to a schedule and a budget.

The usual format for a schedule is to have the name of the production company at the top of the page; this establishes to whom the schedule belongs. This is followed by the working title of the production, which may or may not be the final title of the film, the draft number of the schedule, which defines the particular version of the schedule, the date of issue of the document and the page number.

Following the titling of the schedule there usually is a line of headings that should include: the DATE, which is the shooting date of the specified part of the script; the SC.No. (Scene numbers), which are the shot numbers from the shooting script; D/N, a note of whether the scene is in the day or night; the SCENE, which defines the sequence in the script to be filmed; the CAST, which lists the characters who appear in the scenes to be filmed; and SP.REQS (Special requirements) which should note any important details without which the scene cannot be completed. Sometimes this last item is divided into two sections one of which is SPECIAL REQUIREMENTS and the other OTHER REQUIREMENTS. The first of these usually applies to the technical needs of the crew, for example it may specify wind machines, smoke, dolly and track, blackouts, sound playback or any particular technical need. The OTHER REQUIREMENT usually relates to items used in the performance, like meals, suitcases, guns and, from the example script above, would include crystal globes and lead boxes. If there are any make-up requirements, such as blood, knife or gunshot wounds or similar details, these will fall within the technical area of 'Special requirements'. However, it should be realized that usually, only exceptional items which fall under 'other requirements' are noted on the schedule as the call sheet will carry the more general information. A balance has to be struck between giving all the information required, and giving too much detail, which may swamp the schedule.

Thus a schedule based on the example script will look something like Figure 8.1.

This is one way to present a schedule. However, as already indicated, there is no definitive way to present a schedule, but there are certain requirements which should be fulfilled.

The first of these is the titling of the document. This is vital for the simple reason that everyone needs to know which paper is being referred to, particularly as a schedule is likely to be updated as further information on the production is confirmed. So, in addition to noting the production company's name and working title of the film the top line includes details of which draft of the schedule it is, the date of the draft and the page number. Another reason is that some of the production staff or other crew members may be working on more than one production during the same period, as may happen in the field of commercials, and if titling the schedule helps individual crew members then this is of benefit to the production manager.

The next requirement is the orderly presentation of the information. It does not matter what the precise order is as long as it is logical and consistent and covers all details that the crew and cast need to know.

Thus the order of Date, Scene Number, Day/Night, Scene including Int/Ext, Cast, Special Requirements at the top of the example schedule

```
FAIRFAX FILM LIMITED
FILM 'WIZARD'   SHOOTING SCHEDULE No:2   DATE:        1
```

DATE	SC. No.	D/N	SCENE	CAST	SP. REQS
WEEK 1 Mon 23rd	3. 4.	D	Ext. FIELDS Nr. SITE Address of location	MELANIE MERLYN	Crystal globe
	34.	D	Ext. STANDING STONE	MERLYN MELANIE	Staff R's staff
	3½:p				
Tue 24th	1. 107. 2:p	D	EXT. SITE OF DIG Address of location	RICHARD MELANIE	3 period cars
Wed 25th	2. 6. 108.	D	Ext. SITE OF DIG Address of location	RICHARD MELANIE JENNY DAVID GEORGIA 2 ARCHAEOLOGISTS	3 period cars Lead box Crystal globe
	2⅛:p				
Thu 26th	9. 13. 16.	D	Int. CHRIS'S OFFICE Shepperton Stage 3	CHRIS RICHARD MELANIE ANDREW PROFESSOR S.	Lead box Crystal globe File folder Phone
	11½:p				
Fri 27th	8.	D	Int. SECURITY OFFICE Shepperton Specified Location	RICHARD MELANIE CHRIS JENNY 3 GUARDS	Melanie's bag
	18.	D.	Int. LABORATORY Shepperton Stage 4	RICHARD MELANIE CHRIS ANDREW 2 TECHNICIANS	Lead box Crystal globe File folder
	4¼:p				
Sat. & Sun. 28th/29th			REST DAYS		

```
Continued...
```

Figure 8.1

could equally well be Date, Sets, Int/Ext, Day/Night, Scene, Cast, Special Requirements, Other Requirements.

Because different productions have different needs it must be realized that every schedule should be tailor-made for the particular film. However, it is usual for the date to be the first item of information and the scene, the scene number, the set and the complementary information usually come in the second group of details, followed by the cast and finally by any particular requirements. How this final section is divided up depends on the complexity of the shoot.

On some schedules the casting for each individual scene is noted; again this is the decision of the individual production manager but the important point to remember is that the information should be clear and comprehensive. Thus, in Figure 8.1, the cast for the two different scenes on the Friday of the schedule has been restated because there is the likelihood that Andrew and the two technicians, in scene 18, will not be called until the afternoon, although the rest of the cast in that scene are wanted for the whole day.

An additional detail, in the example above, is the number of pages of script covered by the scenes. This is noted on the final line of each section (3½:p, 2:p, etc.) and is a guide to how much of the script has to be covered. Pages are divided into eighths, and the individual totals on the schedule should add up to the same number of pages in the whole script. This information provides a way of checking that the schedule covers the whole script and also gives an indication of how much work may be required on any one day, by giving a rough timing for the scenes to be covered.

The usual guideline for timing a script is based on a page a minute. So it can be seen in Figure 8.1 that the schedule for Thursday, noting twelve pages of script, may need further consideration. Part of this evaluation will be based on the shooting script and what is demanded from the scene. If the twelve pages are full of action then a 1 day schedule is overly optimistic, but if the twelve pages are full of dialogue and no intricate camera movement is planned then all these scenes may be well within the time allowed.

The opposite can also be true. In the script for John Milius' film *The Wind and the Lion* there was a scene which was simply described by the terms 'There is a battle.' This short line covers an extensive amount of work and clearly the page length is no guide to the time involved in getting the sequence on to the screen—hence the need for careful evaluation of the script.

It should be remembered that well-planned productions and professional crews can shoot a lot of screen time provided the set-ups are not too complex. For example, a common schedule for a filmed television series is a week for each episode; in other words 30 minutes or a third of a feature film a week. In order to achieve this level of turnover, careful planning has to be exercised. One of the schemes used is for the unit to shoot each episode with different key personnel appointed to each episode. Thus there will be a different director, production manager and first assistant for perhaps the first three or four episodes, before the first team returns to manage their second programme. This leap-frogging process will continue until the series is finished. A second unit will cover the stunt work, car chases and any other material which does not involve key cast.

The second way of increasing turnover time is by simplifying the shooting pattern. Crane and tracking shots take time to prepare, so if the number of this kind of shot is reduced then, correspondingly, time will be saved. Of course it is true that modern equipment, like louma cranes and steadicams, will allow craning and tracking shots to be achieved with more ease and a consequent time saving. However, it should be understood that part of the time consumed in filming such shots concerns choreographing the movements of all the elements, namely the actors, the crew and their equipment, and this choreography is equally time consuming almost regardless of the complexity of the equipment.

A third way of reducing time spent is to use more than one camera. At its most common this is the second unit which, as mentioned above, films stunts, scenery, locations and any material which requires no direct directoral control. The other occasions when multi-camera filming is required are for large crowd or battle scenes or crashes or other stunts which cannot easily be repeated. One of the factors which decides when more than one crew is required is the cost. For example, the expense of shooting a scene of some 'soldiers' attacking a fort in the face of gunfire can be enormous. The time taken planning all the explosions, rehearsing the crowd artists, and preparing the crew will be on such a high level that the cost of hiring a second, third or fourth camera and crew will be, relatively speaking, far cheaper than staging a second take. Another instance where second takes are uneconomic is where a crash is required. Cars falling down mountains or trains being derailed are too expensive in time, and sometimes money, for the effect to be missed and therefore three or four cameras will provide the necessary cover both to guarantee that the event is filmed and to give the editor some choices in the cutting. In both of these examples the production manager should expect to spend a lot of time in preparation and the advice of special effects specialists should be heeded, particularly in matters of safety, because a hurried shoot that goes wrong is always more expensive than using more time to get the shot right on the first take.

A final option for saving time is to shoot on 16 mm, or super 16 mm, and blow the result up to 35 mm for distribution purposes. The former film is more than adequate for a programme intended for television or video release but 35 mm is generally required for the cinema. The reason why the smaller format saves time is because the equipment is lighter, which means it is easier to move, uses simpler and lighter cranes and dollies, and in turn results in quicker set-ups. This option is the producer's decision but, depending on contractual requirements, may not be available.

The factor which will have the most influence on the schedule, to the exclusion of anything else is the approved budget. If a budget will only allow for a 10 week shoot and if the first draft schedule comes out at 11 weeks, then some decisions have to be made for reducing the shooting time and this is best done by simplifying the production. Even if the first draft comes out at 10 weeks it still needs to be looked at again with the aim of incorporating some slack time to allow for contingencies, if this spare time is not already in the schedule.

Good production managers will always incorporate some extra space into the schedule and this is generally known as pick-up time. This is not simply a matter of adding a few days on to the end of the schedule. Pick-up time has to be integrated into the whole schedule so that there are opportunities throughout the shoot to catch up. This is particularly necessary where the filming is going to be complex. Pick-up time has to be taken while the unit is on the set or location of the moment. It is always good for crew morale if there is an early wrap but it is very bad for the production's morale if the whole shooting match has to return to a location everyone thought was completed, for a minor pick-up.

The scheduling of pick-up time may seem an overly cautious approach but when it is recalled that every film is a prototype and, in common with the making of any prototype, there will almost certainly be some hitch in the production, then time has to be allowed for these problems to be solved. Besides which there is always a tendency to be overoptimistic about how easy a sequence may be to shoot, so a degree of caution in the schedule will always pay dividends, particularly in dealing with the hitches which will certainly arise.

Sometimes there are factors over which the production has limited or no control. Probably the most common uncontrollable factor is the weather. It has been said that Britain is unique because it is the only country in the world that can have all four seasons in the same day, and the simple point here is that schedules have to plan for just this kind of uncertainty.

If locations cannot be guaranteed to perform in accordance with the script (the Sahara is usually sunny and the Antarctic is always covered by snow), then some preparation has to be made to cover for the days when the conditions required by the script are not available. As has already been mentioned David Lean's production of *Ryan's Daughter* often had two alternative schedules which were drawn up in accordance with the expected weather and the final decision was made on the day of the shoot. This solution is expensive and the size of budget which allows two or more schedules is usually not possible.

Therefore some thought has to be put into considering what options are available whenever variable factors have to be faced. The first point to decide on is the size of the problem. For example, if a film is shot entirely outside then the production manager needs to review the options available for overcoming the problems that an all-exterior shoot will present and this mainly will be the weather. The choices can range from going to a location where the weather is guaranteed, through having a longer schedule or more flexible agreement with the crew and actors so that shooting can take place whenever the weather allows to insuring against adverse conditions, or some combination of all these options or whatever other alternatives may present themselves. All these possible solutions will have some effect on the cost of the film, usually by increasing it, but this effect is minimal when compared with the money that would be wasted if only nine-tenths of the film is shot and some vital scenes are not completed because space has not been allowed for in the schedule to accommodate the variables, whatever they are.

If the production is half interior and half exterior then a variable like the weather can be more easily dealt with by the use of 'cover sets' or by positive scheduling such as filming all the exteriors first and arranging to retreat to interior filming if it is adverse, but this still requires careful planning. The interior and exterior locations have to be close to each other, the right cast has to be available for either option and the interior location has to be ready to accept the crew at short notice. These choices will still have cost considerations.

Thus a main determining factor for deciding which alternative is chosen will be the budget. However, with proper planning, it should be possible to allow for all sorts of alterations when scheduling for a feature film.

The scheduling of a documentary presents some different problems.

CHAPTER 9

SCHEDULING FOR DOCUMENTARIES

Scheduling for any film is essentially the same process, that is the organization of the time needed to complete the shooting of the film as economically as possible. This simply means that the schedule is the 'time budget' for the film.

However, just as scheduling a feature film has its own particular needs and solutions, the scheduling of a documentary presents its own special problems. Initially there are two major differences from the scheduling of a feature film.

The first is in the amount of information available about the production. Because documentaries usually do not have a full script available at the beginning of the shoot but often only a structure or outline of what is wanted, the schedule may only include these basic details until the rest of the information becomes available to be put in place. This should not present a problem for a production manager because documentary crews are much smaller than feature crews, often only eight or nine people compared with the fifty, sixty or more on a feature shoot, and as such it is much easier to keep the unit informed of any late changes or alterations as they occur.

The size of the crew is the indirect cause of the second major difference. Because the production office is smaller, often only the director, the producer or production manager and a production assistant with researchers pursuing their own responsibilities, there is seldom time or opportunity, particularly on difficult locations, to produce daily call sheets and the other information which is essential on a feature shoot. Therefore the schedule often acts as call sheet and a general information carrier about the production in the usual expectation that there will be no time to disseminate this kind of detail during the shoot. Of course it can be suggested that the production office should employ additional production staff and, where the budget allows it, this may well be the best solution. However, it must be appreciated that often the budget on a documentary is too tight for large crews, so the only compromise open to a production manager is to make available all the information collected and collated by the production office before the shoot begins.

However, if all the information is not available it will be realized that preparing a fully detailed schedule will not be possible even if this is the ideal to aim for. It may be wondered why it is not possible for all the information to be immediately available and the answer to this depends on the subject being filmed. Wildlife documentaries are a classic case where material has to be shot as the opportunity presents itself, sometimes on the run, sometimes after weeks of patient waiting. The 'Fly on the wall' documentary is another area where material has to be grabbed whenever possible and therefore cannot be readily scheduled. For example, a documentary about fire fighters will be enhanced by film of the subjects at work, extinguishing a fire, but the crew will have to wait for the emergency to be called and this means the schedule has to be very flexible.

An example of a schedule is shown in Figure 9.1, which displays the basic information for the whole of the first week's schedule, essentially covering those items which remain constant throughout the shoot.

Any information which is not immediately available should be noted with 't.b.a.' (to be advised), showing that further information is going to be added to the schedule in the future. The rest of the schedule is made up in a similar pattern to a feature schedule.

```
"COMPANY' SHOOTING SCHEDULE — 'TITLE SOMETIME'
Third draft — date
WEEK A. Monday 5th–Friday 9th
'OFFICE' SHOOT

                    GENERAL INFORMATION

SCHEDULE: The dates for this schedule are fixed as above but,
   within these dates, the schedule is still open to amendment and
   should not be accepted as totally fixed.
KEY CAST: Any cast who appear in more than one scene will need to
   have change of costume, e.g. extra shirts, ties and jackets.
COLOUR CODING: In order to distinguish between locations predomi-
   nant colours are specified and sets will be dressed in the
   appropriate colour as much as possible but not exclusively so.
```

This item was peculiar to this particular production, but it indicates the individuality of every production, the need for information and the fact that there is no 'right' way to draw up a documentary schedule.

```
FACILITIES: Space should be provided round each location so that
   the camera has room to track and move round the scene.
   There will be occasions when lights need to be placed outside
   windows and cable access will need to be available.
   The in-house electrician will need to be available.
   One or two trolleys will be needed to move equipment from loca-
   tion to location.
```

LOCATIONS: Locations are specified for each scene but additional
shots may be required in the reception lobby, library, restaurant, large ground-floor meeting room with window blinds and the
meeting room in the canteen block.
The quietest of the meeting rooms may well be needed for extra
sound recording of dialogue, usually at the end of each day.
Can the availability of the VDU area for filming be confirmed?
VISUAL AIDS: Anything which assists the visual images in each
scene will be welcomed as a positive suggestion.
SHOOTING: The usual shooting time will be between 8.30 a.m. and
5.00 p.m.
Lunch will be taken in conjunction with 'Company's' timetable
whenever possible.
There may be one evening shot for a 'late-night think-tank ses-
sion'this will be confirmed nearer the shoot.
'COMPANY' CONTACT: PRO *Contact name*
'Company', *address, post code, phone no.*
ROUTE: The following are suggested routes to the 'Company' start-
ing from the M4 in West London:
Route A: Take M4 to Bristol, there turn north on to M5 at junc-
tion 20.
Leave M5 at junction ...
The approximate distance by this route is 190 miles.
Route B: Take M4 to Swindon, junction 15, there turn north on
to the A419 to Cirencester. At Cirencester ...
The approximate distance for this route is 100 miles.
ACCOMMODATION: The accommodation is at a local hotel and comprises
single rooms with private facilities and includes breakfast.
Dinner is additional. The production will pick up the meal
bills, up to the value of £XX, but no drinks bills.

Another option is for the production to pay a fixed evening meal
allowance. There is an agreed minimum rate but often productions will
pay above this minimum.

The address of the accommodation is:
Name of hotel, address, post code, phone no.
To reach the hotel from the 'Company':
Leave the 'Company' and go straight over the first junction and
at the next roundabout take the third left to ... . The hotel
is on the right-hand side of the road.
The total distance is about 5 miles.

CREW:	Director	*Name*	*Address*	*Phone no.*
	Production Manager	*Name*	*Address*	*Phone no.*
	Production Assistant	*Name*	*Address*	*Phone no.*
	Camera	*Name*	*Address*	*Phone no.*
	Camera Assistant	*Name*	*Address*	*Phone no.*
	Sound	t.b.a.		
	Sparks	*Name*	*Address*	*Phone no.*
	Grip	*Name*	*Address*	*Phone no.*

If there are any queries on this schedule please contact the production manager
Name — Phone no.

Figure 9.1

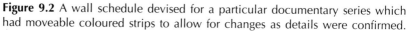

Figure 9.2 A wall schedule devised for a particular documentary series which had moveable coloured strips to allow for changes as details were confirmed.

Some of the schedule information may apparently be 'teaching grandma to suck eggs' but it must be remembered that many documentary shoots will be coming into contact with people who do not know anything about the film-making process and therefore need to be told everything. Part of good management, in any sphere, is ensuring that the individuals involved in whatever project understand clearly what they have to do because worried or ill-informed people do not perform well.

The schedule for the week should be laid out in a similar fashion to Figure 9.3.

A point to notice in this example schedule is that Friday afternoon is not specified for a particular scene and alternative options have been offered for additional filming.

The reason for leaving the Friday afternoon schedule open ended is so that any time lost during the week can be recovered but, at the same time, the suggested alternatives allow for filming at other locations and a consequent saving of time on later schedules.

It can be seen from the schedule that the same pattern of information is given for each day: the day and date with the day being split into two parts. The scene numbers and title are indicated so that everyone can read in the script what is wanted and this is followed by a brief explanation. Then the place, the people and particular requirements are noted and if nothing is required this too should be stated so that everyone

```
SCHEDULE — No.3          'TITLE SOMETIME'          DATE:
```

MON. a.m. Travel from London to 'Company', Oxford.
5th

Depart London to arrive at 'Company' by 11.00 a.m.

p.m. Sc.12. INTRODUCTION TO 'COMPANY'.

A series of exterior shots to introduce 'Company'.

LOCATION: Ext. 'Company', including entrance.

CAST: No specific.

PROPS: No specific.

REQUIRE: The sign at the front entrance to be refurbished and any missing letters replaced.

Sc.18 DESIGN DISCUSSIONS.

This sequence is intended to show that the design process is discussed during informal meetings and is a continuing process.

LOCATION: Ext. The 'Chestnut avenue' on the south side of the 'Company' office and, if time is available, the Ints in the restaurant, reception lobby or library.

CAST: *Names*

PROPS: No specific.

REQUIRE: Costume changes.

TUE. a.m. Scs 11 & 12A. A VERY EARLY PROJECT MEETING.
6th

This is a reconstruction of one of the early A2 rig project group meetings.

LOCATION: Int. C.B.'s area.

CAST: *Names*

PROPS: Copy of report 'Requirements for Mk A2 RIG'.

Mock up if original not available.

Any other relevant visual aids, e.g. model of Mk 1 Rig and any drawings.

REQUIRE: Plenty of room needed round the meeting table.

No particular colour emphasis.

p.m. Sc.21. EARLY RADIATOR MEETING.

This is a meeting of the designers with the radiator specialist.

LOCATION: Int. NW corner of 'Company' office. Heather view.

CAST: *Names*

PROPS: Any visual aids. Particularly section drawings of valves and seals.

REQUIRE: Space for tracking.

Colour code blue, so additional screens should be of this colour.

EXPECT TO RIG FOR Sc.15 AT THE END OF THE DAY.

FRI. p.m. Dependent on progress during the previous 4 days this
9th   afternoon will be used for:

    A. Completion of Company shoot.

    B. Exteriors at Totleigh Towers: Scs. 3, 5, 25.

    C. Completion of Cheese shoot.

Figure 9.3

```
DRAFT  SCHEDULE  3          'TITLE SOMETIME'              DATE:

WEEK B.
CUMBRIA SHOOT

DAY -1   Travel to Cumbria, and check in to accommodation the day
         before shooting commences, Time to get to the Columbia
         engineering works in Cumbria from London, approximately 5½
         hours.
DAY 1    The Columbia engineering works. Scs 39, 40.
         a.m.  Raw casting and welding in the heavy engineering
               shop.
         p.m.  Polishing and insulating.
DAY 2    a.m.  Ram borer.
         p.m.  Rig assembly, detailed assembly shots.
               Can this be done in the heavy engineering shop?
DAY 3    a.m.  A finished rig going into the paint shop.
         p.m.  A painted rig.
NOTE:    During days 2 & 3, dependent on the weather, scs 49, 50
         at Emmerdale and the road to Emmerdale will be shot. This
         is an evening shot and half an hour is needed to reach
         the location. Or possibly the village of Seaford.


CHANGE ACCOMMODATION TO SEAFORD.

DAY 4    a.m.  Sc.38. Filming on BR flat roller. Between Ware and
               Seaford. There will be a need to stop the train from
               time to time.
         p.m.  Scs 41, 42, 46. Seaford shunting yard. The cover
               taken off the flat roller and the moving of the rig
               up to the fuel handling complex. Camera requires
               afternoon shooting for the train at the works.
         EVENING: Sc.48. Script character leaving work. Passing main
               gate.
DAY 5    a.m.  Sc.47. Locker room at the end of the day.
               Overhead shot from bridge between office and works.
         p.m.  Return to London.
```

Figure 9.4

realizes the blank is intended and not a typing error. It does not really matter what pattern is used as long as it is logical and consistent, although the basic questions of when, where, who and what are the ones to be answered and are usually asked in that order, and it will be seen that this order is similar to the one used in the examples above for feature schedules.

If the whole production is not completed in one shoot it is of benefit to attach at this stage an outline schedule for the rest of the shoot. No specific dates need be given but there should be an indication of the likely activities for each day. This results in an addition to the schedule which may look like Figure 9.4.

Again the third week, week C, will be laid out in a similar fashion.

REQUIREMENTS FOR SHOOTING

Before shooting at 'Company' can begin:

The sign outside the front entrance should be cleaned.

The following staff should be available during the shooting period:

Before shooting at the engineering works can begin:

We will need a completely raw casting available.

One completed rig, except for painting.

One painted rig, to be held over for the film.

Rigs in different stages of construction.

Meeting with company safety officer.

The 'Company' inspector, to be available.

Before filming at Seaford can begin:

A completed rig should be available for the unit's use over the 2 days of the shoot.

Liaison with BR needs to be confirmed for use of a locomotive to bring a flat roller along the line.

Before filming at Totleigh can begin:

An A2 rig should be available for the unit's use over the shooting period. A low loader should also be available to the unit.

An engineer, probably KS., should be available for the production.

Briefing of company safety instructions.

PRODUCTION INFORMATION/REQUIREMENTS:

In addition to the standard equipment, the following will be required:

at the Columbia engineering works

for cameraman: 2 X B guns - smoke
                 2 Windbags + black material
                 Pre-hook up 13 amp power point

for prod.man.:   Measuring instruments

at 'Company':

for cameraman: Note fluorescent tubes are 85 W natural light tubes.
                 Suction mount for truck.
                 Lights for hall areas — 4 par blue
                                       — 4 par tungsten

at ALL LOCATIONS

for prod.man.:   two walkie-talkies.

TRANSPORT: Production manager to provide production vehicle.
                 'Company' to provide camera car.

CONTACTS: At Columbia: *Name*   *Phone no.*
                                 Name   *Phone no.*
                 At 'Company':   *Name*   *Phone no.*
                 [This is a list of everyone who might need to be contacted during the production and their telephone number together with a note of where they work.]

THIS SCHEDULE IS STILL OPEN TO ALTERATIONS WITHIN ANY INDIVIDUAL WEEK - AT THE MOMENT WE EXPECT TO SHOOT WEEKS A & B IN THE LATE SUMMER AND WEEK C IN THE FOLLOWING SPRING. (The dates will be confirmed as soon as possible; dependent on Columbia's schedule.)

Figure 9.5

The first step in the preparation of a schedule would be very much in the form outlined in Figure 9.4, and the fuller schedule would be detailed on to this skeleton.

Finally a list of general information is included with instructions for actions to be taken, details to be researched, specialized equipment required and any other information that the production manager needs to impart in order that the shoot will go smoothly as shown in Figure 9.5. One of the most important areas to be noted as this stage is the health and safety rules to be observed, such as hard-hat instructions, no smoking areas, access details and any other information which the crew need to know for its security.

This final page, which would be compiled from notes made during the pre-production location reconnaissance, is a checklist of various items and requirements which have to be available or fulfilled if the schedule is going to be maintained. Documentaries are often filmed on locations where other people are working and, in these situations, anyone not immediately involved in the production of the film will not necessarily give the film the same priority as the production crew although the production will be relying on them to do certain tasks before shooting can begin. Therefore the production office and the contact at the location in question need to keep in touch and ensure that the work requested has been done before the unit arrives to film. As with most management problems the key tool for providing a solution is communication, keeping in touch with what is happening and making sure that it is happening.

Once the schedule has been drafted the budget can be checked against its demands although it must be remembered that it is the budget which usually has the controlling or final say on the shape of a schedule. Therefore careful and proper budgeting is a vital ingredient to good production management.

CHAPTER 10

BUDGETING FOR FEATURES

The budget is one of the key documents in any project and particularly so in film production, especially in the realm of feature films where costs sometimes reach what appear to be extraordinary levels. Consequently a proper understanding of how costs are arrived at is essential.

Generally speaking the calculation of the initial budget is not the job of the production manager. However, this is not to say a production manager will not be involved in working out costings for a possible project in the very early stages, because of the usual 'chicken or egg' situation that arises at the conception of a film.

Almost always the first question asked of a film maker presenting a script or proposal is how much is it going to cost to make the film? To provide an answer to this question a budget has to be prepared. This in turn presents the question who is going to pay the person who calculates the budget, particularly if the money has not yet been raised? This is an eternal problem for the producer and especially for the producer of a first-time feature but, regardless of how this problem is solved, there will come a time, which should be early in the pre-production phase, when the production manager will see the draft budget.

Seeing the budget means an understanding is needed of how it is made up. This is because a proper evaluation of the cost of the production has to be arrived at. During the period of production a proper control must be kept over the finances and this can only be done if the production manager appreciates how the figures were arrived at in the first instance.

Before considering an example budget an understanding of the way a feature budget is laid out is needed. The standard form produced by the old National Film Finance Corporation (NFFC) in collaboration with the Guild of Film Production Accountants & Financial Administrators is the document used by most people working in the British feature industry. Individual companies, like the major American production houses and some television companies, produce their own forms but, in essence, there are only variations on a theme and the basic structure in all cases is very much the same. The next point to realize is that if all the information requested in a budget form is supplied correctly then, regardless of the size of the film, all the items needed for the costing of the production will have been covered and an accurate budget should have been achieved.

The NFFC/Guild of Film Production Accountants form

This form is of considerable length. It will be used as a guide for a feature production budget. It follows the practice of titling a document with the name of the production company and the title of the film. The rest of the first page of the form covers the expected schedule of the production and a list of the sources of finance and deferments (in order of repayment). It also notes the details of the delivery date, running time, Completion Guarantor(s) and on which draft of the script the budget is based.

This last point is very important as scripts often go through more than one drafting and every version will have a positive or negative effect on the budget. The rule of thumb for the shooting of a feature script is about a page a minute. Therefore a feature script should be 90–120 pages long. The first draft of *Gone with the Wind* was some 300 pages long, so the producer, David O. Selznick, decided to take it in hand. After some months of work he produced a second draft which was even longer than the first and much longer than the final screenplay on which the 220 minute film was finally budgeted. This simply shows that things do not always go the way intended.

The next page of the form is the budget summary. This is established so that the costs for the major stages in production can be seen separately. These are: preparation and tests, locations, main shooting studio and lot, music, dubbing post sync. and effects, finishing costs and the total. This page is a basic form of cash flow for the production and will give the producer and the financier an idea of how much money is needed at any one stage of the proceedings. A more detailed cash flow will be needed if proper control over the budget is to be maintained but the detail will depend on the size of the production and the requirements of the financing organization.

The major sections of the form

As well as being divided into columns (see Figure 10.1 for an example page), the form is also divided into three horizontal sections; there are the 'above the line' costs, the 'below the line' costs and the indirect costs.

'Above the line' costs include the fees for the story and script and for key personnel, director, producer and stars. These figures are part of the budget but generally do not have a direct effect upon the actual cost of making the film, as usually they are covered in the fee for the production

N — HOTEL & LIVING EXPENSES *continued*

	Details	Rate	Preparations and Tests		Locations		Main Shooting Studio and Lot		Music		Dubbing Post-Synch. and Effects		Finishing Costs		TOTAL
			Wks.	Amount	Wks.	Amount	Wks.	Amount	Wks.	Amount	Wks.	Amount	Wks.	Amount	
2	**Other Living Expenses**														
	Foreign Artistes, etc., Expenses														
	Studio Trolley Service														
	Unit Meal Allowances														
	TOTAL														

O — INSURANCES

	Details
1	Pre-Production Indemnity
2	Film Producers' Indemnity
3	Consequential Loss
4	Abandonment Risk Extension
5	Errors & Omissions
6	Negative & Daily Takes
7	Employers' Liability
8	Public Liability—Third Party
9	Equipment
10	Sets, Wardrobe and Properties
11	Action Vehicles
12	Cash in Transit
13	Accountant—Fidelity Guarantee
14	Unit Personal Accident, etc.
	TOTAL

P — SOCIAL SECURITY: HOLIDAY AND SICK PAY SURCHARGES

	Details	Rate
1	**Salaried Staff**	
	(a) Hol. Credits Prodn. Co. Staff	% of £
	(b) N.H.I. Prodn. Co. Staff (incl. Grad. Ins.)	% of £
	(c) Studio Surcharge	% of £
2	**Manual Labour**	
	Studio Surcharge	% of £
3	**Artistes and Crowd**	
	N.H.I.	% of £
	TOTAL	

24

Figure 10.1

as a whole. This can be best explained by realizing that to have Robert Redford or Meryl Streep in a film will add a figure of about $4 million for either artiste in the 'above the line' section of the budget. However, the same film can be made with any actor or actress who, because they are unknown, will simply receive a salary and this salary may well be accounted for in the 'below the line' part of the budget. The production will now cost X million pounds or dollars less although the actual cost of filming will be the same.

The 'below the line' costs are the estimated actual costs of the film. In this part of the budget any change in the time, any alteration in the film stock requirements, any addition to or subtraction from the cast, crew or equipment, in fact any change in the perceived needs of the production, will be reflected in the cost.

The final section, the indirect costs, are items which are either ongoing, like office overheads, or related to the above and below line costs, like the completion guarantor's fee.

The final budget is the sum of these three parts.

Specific sections of the form

The individual parts of the budget form are divided into sections which are usually categorized by letters and, where necessary, split into numbered subsections.

The first section, A, covers STORY AND SCRIPT rights, that is the writer's fees including living expenses and costing for script typing and duplicating. Subsection B covers the PRODUCER'S and DIRECTOR'S FEES, and subsection C the PRODUCTION UNIT SALARIES, this latter item being divided into several subsections. Item D covers ART DEPARTMENT SALARIES and item E, for the costs for ARTISTES, is divided into subsection 1, the 'above the line' costs, and subsection 1a, the 'below the line' costs. This section extends to stand-ins, doubles, stunt personnel, chaperones, crowds and other artistes.

Section F, MUSICAL DIRECTION, MUSICIANS, ETC., includes a subsection on copyright and performing rights, section G, concerns COSTUMES AND WIGS, and section H, MISCELLANEOUS PRODUCTION STORES (EXCLUDING SETS), generally covers items like camera tape, gels, spare bulbs, spacing and anything else which is purchased for the production rather than hired.

Section I concerns FILM AND LABORATORY CHARGES and covers the purchase of negative stock, processing, printing and editing phases of laboratory work up to the delivery of the final answer print.

STUDIO RENTALS, section J, covers the hire of studio space and all the other associated facilities like dubbing theatres and cutting rooms which are traditionally part of a studio complex. With the current trend for independent productions to be filmed on location and not to use a studio it should be realized that facilities like offices, cutting rooms and dubbing theatres are often rented or hired individually. However, they still come under this part of the budget.

When considering studio rentals the production manager should find out what else can be provided by the studio for the production. Often the benefits of working out of a studio and having these facilities close to hand during the production, even if the studio stages are not being used, far outweigh any supposed saving in cost by renting a cheaper cutting room some distance from the other necessary post-production facilities.

Sections K and L cover EQUIPMENT hire and POWER. The equipment is divided into camera equipment, lighting equipment, sound equipment, grip equipment, cutting room equipment and miscellaneous equipment; this last subsection includes items hired for the production office, like word processors or polaroid cameras.

Section M covers TRAVEL AND TRANSPORT. In terms of good budgeting this section can be very hard to estimate correctly and if overestimation is going to be made in any part of a budget this is the place to be generous. The usual reason for underestimating this section is a failure to appreciate how many miles are travelled by a crew during a production particularly in the simple day-to-day running backwards and forwards on a location and in the use of messengers who, if required at short notice, are often very expensive. An editor in a cutting room using one messenger bike a day for the whole of the editing period can add a noticeable sum to the cost of a film.

Section N covers HOTEL AND LIVING EXPENSES. This is another area of the budget which can prove to be expensive. One reason is because if accommodation is not sorted out soon enough a late booking usually results in having to accept prices higher than initially budgeted. Another reason is that it is often forgotten that the production continues after the shoot has ended and the editors and other post-shooting personnel may have living expenses which need to be budgeted for.

INSURANCES are covered under section O and the list tabulated in the budget form is a good guideline for the insurance policies which may be required by any production.

Section P covers SOCIAL SECURITY: HOLIDAY AND SICK PAY SURCHARGES. The precise calculations should be done with the advice of a production accountant, particularly as the production company will have different responsibilities for different technicians depending on whether they are freelance or employees of the production company, but, for the purpose of preparing a budget, 25% of the salary bill can give a rough guide of the likely final figure for the production.

An area of the budget often overlooked is section Q, namely PUBLICITY SALARIES AND EXPENSES. Even the best films need some publicity to whet the audience's appetite and some backers demand a certain level of publicity as part of the contract.

The subsections in the MISCELLANEOUS EXPENSES, section R, include an allowance for the post-production scripts, the censor's fees, medical fees and location first aid. The production office expenses are also part of this section and include telephones, postage, printing and stationery and any other office needs apart from the office rentals which should be accounted for in section J. There are fees and levies to be paid to various professional bodies, like the Film Producers' Association of Great Britain, and training schemes, like Jobfit. These expenses generally are required under the relevant production agreements.

The next five pages of the form cover section S, SETS AND MODELS, and section T, SPECIAL EFFECTS. Both these sections require the advice of relevant specialists if a realistic figure is going to be arrived at.

The final page of the budget form includes section U, SPECIAL LOCATION FACILITIES, and the indirect costs of FINANCE AND LEGAL CHARGES, section Y, and OVERHEADS, section Z. In section Y there is a line for the completion guarantee fee which is usually 6% of the above and below line sections of the budget. This may be reduced when the Guarantor is dealing with a Producer who has a good track record. It should be understood that a Financier almost certainly will not back a production without a guarantee.

Essentially, the completion guarantee or bond promises the backer that the film will be finished, come what may. However, before giving such an assurance, the completion guarantor will need to be confident that the production is properly set up and well managed. In order to establish this confidence the guarantor will want to approve the script, budget and schedule, and also have some say about the crewing and casting of the production. Once this is approved the guarantor will keep a close eye on the day to day progress of the production. It can be clearly seen that these are one set of reasons why a production has to be well managed.

In section Z the production company's overheads are intended to recognize the producer's expenditure on projects which have not come to fruition.

After the main body of the form there are a couple of APPENDIX pages for the analysis of set costs and wardrobe costs. Often there are blank pages of schedule which can be used if a particular section requires more space.

In most of the form the majority of the sections are laid out in the same way. They cover the rate for each item followed by columns for the costing of the preparation and test period, the location filming period, the studio shooting period, the music, the dubbing and post-syncing and effects periods, the finishing costs and finally the total for each line. Each column will also result in a total and these totals are the basis for a cash flow for the production. The cash flow has an importance related to budget control and this will be looked at in greater detail in Chapter 12.

DRAFT BUDGET SUMMARY

A completed draft summary, based on the example feature script, may look something like Figure 10.2. This example budget highlights a number of points. The first point of interest for any financier to note is

```
DRAFT BUDGET                    'WIZARD'                DATE:
```

(1) 'ABOVE THE LINE' COSTS:		
A Story and script	£	65 400
B Producer's fee	£	155 000
Director's fee	£	55 000
E Principal artistes	£	90 000
	£	365 400
(2) 'BELOW THE LINE' COSTS:		
C Production unit salaries;		
1 Production manager & secretaries	£	70 000
2 Assistant director & continuity	£	35 000
3 Technical advisers (inc. choreographer's)	£	5000
4 Camera crews	£	55 500
5 Sound crews	£	14 000
6 Editing staff	£	85 000
7 Stills camera staff	£	8000
8 Wardrobe staff	£	25 000
9 Make-up artists	£	14 000
10 Hairdressers	£	12 000
11 Casting	£	9000
12 Production accountancy	£	45 000
13 Projectionists	£	500
14 Miscellaneous studio staff	£	1000
15 Foreign unit technicians	£	—
D Art department salaries	£	35 000
E Artistes:		
1 Cast (other than principals)	£	72 000
2 Stand-ins, doubles, stuntmen	£	10 000
3 Crowd	£	45 000
F Music, direction, musicians	£	6500
G Costumes and wigs	£	43 000
H Misc. production stores	£	18 000
I Film stock & lab. charges	£	132 000
J Studio rentals	£	96 000
K Equipment	£	69 500
L Power	£	3700
M Travel & transport:		
1 Location	£	60 000
2 Studio	£	19 000
N Hotel and living expenses:		
1 Location	£	159 600
2 Studio	£	5500
O Insurances	£	36 000
P Social security etc.	£	143 700
Q Publicity salaries & expenses	£	8800
R Miscellaneous expenses	£	141 200
S Sets & models:		
1 Labour - construction	£	28 000
1a Materials - construction	£	44 000
2 Labour - dressing	£	27 000
3 Labour - operating	£	22 000
4 Labour - striking	£	9900
5/6 Labour - lighting & lamp spotting	£	18 900
7 Labour - foreign unit	£	—
8 Properties	£	35 000
T Special effects	£	38 400
U Special location facilities	£	32 500
TOTAL 'BELOW THE LINE' COST	£	1 739 700
(3) INDIRECT COSTS:		
Y Finance & legal	£	145 000
Z Overheads	£	186 000
TOTAL INDIRECT COST	£	331 000
TOTAL (1+2+3)	£	2 436 100

Figure 10.2

the total budget. In this case it will be realized that this is not a big-budget film and the above the line costs will show that there are no megastars involved.

Other information that can be quickly culled from the figures indicates that there is minimal foreign travel, if any, but there certainly is some studio filming contemplated and the size of the costume budget could indicate that production is probably covering a subject which is wider than a simple contemporary drama.

Some of the expenditure in items A and B of the budget form will be part of the development costs and, depending on how and where this money was raised, it may well have to be returned before the completion of the production. Monies from the National Film Development Fund together with a premium on the loan are usually repaid on the first day of principal photography and consequently this requirement has to be allowed for in the original budgeting.

A further factor to look at is the percentage or proportion that each section takes of the budget as a whole. The crew costs for example are between a fifth and a sixth of the budget, whereas the stock and laboratory costs are about a fifteenth to a twentieth of the budget. Other sections, like Artistes, Music, Travel and Transport, Hotel and Living Expenses, and Sets and Models, will vary much more widely because they depend on individual script requirements, but these proportions should be kept in mind because they all relate to each other.

There is a popular misconception that the crew can always do one more take because film stock is the cheapest item on the set. This is not true because one more take involves more than the cost of the stock going through the camera. There is the additional time involved for the hire of equipment and the work of the performers and crew. This latter point extends to the editor, because every printed take has to be synchronized, looked at and evaluated; all this requires time and if the extra take results in overtime payments this too is an additional cost, so even if the price of the stock used in the extra take is minimal the resultant effect on the production will not necessarily be so.

A final point to note is that the lowest unit in this draft budget is a hundred; there is no benefit in calculating a detailed figure for some parts of the budget when it is not possible to do so for others. Also, a figure calculated to the nearest penny will certainly be wrong unless it is a fixed fee for the whole production, and therefore there is no point in making the effort. A feature budget is sufficiently accurate at the nearest hundred and if a calculation comes out to units of pounds and pence or dollars and cents it should be rounded up to the next hundred or two hundred. The agreed final budget may well be to the nearest unit, pound or dollar, but the reality of a production is that a precise figure is unlikely to be met at the final accounting. However, this does not mean that no effort should be made to produce a budget which is as accurate as possible.

The need for precision is even more necessary for the documentary budget.

CHAPTER 11

BUDGETING FOR DOCUMENTARIES

Budgeting for a documentary production essentially involves the same process as budgeting for a feature film. The same form can be used although individual sponsors, usually television companies, may have their own forms. The main difference between the two budgets will be the size of the final figure and therefore it is important to understand how these figures are arrived at.

The first factor which has an effect on the budget is the agreement under which the film is being produced. The union and the Employers' Association have signed a freelance production agreement. Part of this agreement covers the crew rates for feature films, and there is a separate scale of rates for documentary productions. This agreement defines the terms and conditions under which the crews will work and the production will be run. These terms are important because of their budgetary implications, and particularly because they include information about working hours, overtime rates, travelling conditions, quality of accommodation, health and safety, and the numerous other items which concern the welfare of working crews.

Copies of the agreement together with the current minimum pay rates are available from the Employers' Association and the union.

With regard to the pay it should be realized that the agreement specifies different rates and these rates are updated every 6 months, to stay in line with inflation. Because the published rates are agreed minimums this means that the going rate for technicians will usually be above the figure in the agreement and therefore the salary eventually noted in the budget will depend on the individual technician. The only way to calculate this figure is to negotiate with the person concerned to find out what their 'going rate' is. Similar negotiations will have to take place with all freelance people involved in the production, the most obvious example being the high fees that the major stars on a feature film can command, but a similar position can be arrived at on a documentary film where a well-known presenter can ask for a proportionally high fee

LABORATORY SERVICES

The Laboratory, located in Perivale, offers a complete film service from negative processing through to bulk release printing for 16mm, Super 16mm, and 35mm film.

Specialist services include printing by total immersion, special effects, and blowing up from 16mm and Super 16mm to 35mm.

Pence per foot unless otherwise stated	16mm Negative	35mm Negative		16mm Negative	35mm Negative
Processing			**Duplicating - Optical**		
Camera Film - All Types	11.10	11.10	35mm Intermediate Positive		190.00
Extended Development	16.25	16.25	from 16mm		
			A & B Roll Printing Add	35.00	35.00
Rush Prints			Check Prints	24.00	24.00
One Light - Whole Roll	23.50	35.00			
Graded	38.50	44.00	**Answer Prints**		
Breakdown Scene Selection					
and Negative Adjustments			First Trial Print		
(per hour)	£27.50	£27.50	(Including effects: fades, dissolves, etc)	57.50	62.50
			A & B Roll (Including Opticals)		
Negative Cutting			Add	9.00	9.00
A & B Per Reel					
(16mm-400' - 35mm-1000')	£270.00	£325.00	**Release Prints**		
Single Roll per reel	£125.00	£225.00	(Excluding Commercials)		
Black Spacing	12.00	16.00	Single Copies	24.00	24.00
			2 - 10 Copies	20.00	20.00
Duplicating - Contact			11 - 19	18.50	18.50
Intermediate Positive or			20 - 49	15.00	15.50
Negative	72.00	113.00	50 and Over	by quotation	
A & B roll Printing Add	27.00	27.00	Sections	33.00	34.00
			A & B Roll Add	9.00	9.00

Minimum Charge £25 on each item.

Figure 11.1a

if he or she is in sufficient demand. However, in terms of budgeting the documentary production does not have an 'above the line' part of the budget.

Having negotiated with each individual, or their agent, the next important action is to get it down as a written agreement.

The costing of processing, equipment hire and the other facilities which are needed is commenced by asking those companies providing the services for their rates. These catalogues provide information in a variety of ways.

Laboratory rates can be laid out in the ways shown in Figure 11.1. It can be seen from these examples that processing is generally quoted in terms of pence per foot. Different parts of each catalogue are given over to different services and amongst the factors which make up the eventual choice of a laboratory will be which of these other services can be provided. An example of stock prices is given in Figure 11.2.

Camera, sound and lighting equipment can be presented in the ways shown in Figure 11.3. Again the catalogues are divided into different sections and the rates are generally presented in terms of daily or weekly

LABORATORY

	Pence per foot unless otherwise stated				Pence per foot unless otherwise stated	
	16mm Negative	35mm Negative			16mm Negative	35mm Negative
Processing			**Duplicating – Optical**			
Camera Film – All Types	9.75	9.75	35mm Intermediate Positive from 16mm			175.00
Extended Development	14.25	14.25	A & B Roll Printing Add		32.00	32.00
			Check Prints		21.50	21.50
Rush Prints						
One Light – Whole Roll	21.00	32.00				
Graded	34.00	40.00	**Answer Prints**			
Breakdown Scene Selection and			First Trial Print		51.50	55.00
Negative Adjustments per hour	£23.50	£23.50	A & B Roll (Including Opticals) Add		8.00	8.00
Negative Cutting						
Chequerboard Per Reel			**Release Prints**			
(16mm-400′ – 35mm-1,000′)	£224.00	£265.00	Single Copies		22.50	22.50
Single Roll per reel		£190.00	2-10 Copies		19.50	19.50
Black Spacing	10.25	14.50	11-19		18.50	18.50
			20-49		14.00	14.00
Duplicating – Contact			50 and Over		By Quotation	
Intermediate Positive or Negative	70.00	104.50	Sections		30.00	35.50
A & B Roll Printing Add	24.00	24.00	A & B Roll Add		8.00	8.00

Minimum Charges 100′ on all items except Developing 200′

ALL PRICES ARE SUBJECT TO V.A.T.

Figure 11.1b

AGFA XT COLOUR NEGATIVE FILM   JULY 1989

16mm Camera Film
XT 125 (125 ASA)   £

| 100ft | (30.5m) | Daylight-Loading Spool | per roll | 14.67 |
| 400ft | (122m) | Wound on core | per roll | 53.83 |

XT 320 (320 ASA)

| 100ft | (30.5m) | Daylight-Loading Spool | per roll | 15.40 |
| 400ft | (122m) | Wound on core | per roll | 56.52 |

35mm Camera Film
XT 125 (125 ASA)

200ft	(61m)	Wound on core	per roll	46.72
400ft	(122m)	Wound on core	per roll	93.44
1000ft	(305m)	Wound on core	per roll	233.60

XT 320 (320 ASA)

200ft	(61m)	Wound on core	per roll	49.06
400ft	(122m)	Wound on core	per roll	98.11
1000ft	(305m)	Wound on core	per roll	245.28

Figure 11.2

		Daily	Weekly
Z54	**PANAFLEX 'X'**	250.00	750.00

Z54 **PANAFLEX 'X'** 250.00 750.00
BNCR MOUNT
c/w 24/25 integral crystal motor, variable
shutter, follow focus control and standard matte
box/lens hood (less magazines, extra matte
boxes and battery complement).
6-32fps variable speed

Z99 **PANAFLEX 'X'** 250.00 750.00
PV MOUNT
with features and accessories as above

P71 **SUPER PSR** P.O.A.
PV MOUNT
c/w 4 x 1000' magazines, 24/25 integral crystal
motor, variable shutter, 24v battery complement,
standard matte box/lens hood, 5 x standard
Panavision spherical lenses (24mm T2.8,
32mm T2.8, 40mm T2, 50mm T2, 75mm T2) and
integral video assist viewfinder.
6-32fps variable speed

P67 **SUPER PSR** P.O.A.
with features and accessories as above.
For anamorphic use but without lenses

Z97 **PVSR** 160.00 480.00
PV MOUNT
c/w 4 x 1000' magazines, Panaspeed crystal
motor, 36v battery complement, standard
matte box/lens hood, 5 x standard Panavision
spherical lenses (24mm T2.8, 32mm T2.8,
40mm T2, 50mm T2, 75mm T2).
12-32fps variable speed

P66 **PVSR** 160.00 480.00
with features and accessories as above. For
anamorphic use but without lenses

Note: All cameras are supplied with changing bag,
waterproof cover, tape measure and power
cables

Figure 11.3a

hire. The daily rate is usually a quarter or a third of the weekly rate and this fact should be remembered when considering how long the shoot should be.

It should be noted that the terms and conditions for the processing of stock or the hire of equipment are usually attached to the rates. If they are not then they should be asked for, understood and agreed before any service is accepted, as should any variation to the published rates. During the budgeting process it should be assumed that no discounts will be negotiated and that the full book rate will have to be paid. Although discounts can be arranged it should be realized that often these

16mm LENSES

		Day	Week
16mm LENS SETS			
XS2	Set of New Zeiss High Speed 12mm, 16mm, 25mm; all T1.3 (Min focus: 12mm, 8″; 16mm, 8″; 25mm, 10″)	54	162
XS1	Set of Zeiss High Speed 12mm, 16mm, 25mm; all T1.3 (Min focus: 12mm, 8″; 16mm, 10″; 25mm, 15″)	51	153
XS5	Set of Cooke Kinetals (for ST only) 12.5mm, 17.5mm, 25mm, 37.5mm; all T2 (Min focus: 12.5mm, 12″; 17.5mm, 12″; 25mm, 12″; 37.5mm, 21″)	13	39
16mm SINGLE LENSES			
XL20	3.5mm Century (fixed focus)	13	39
XL1	5.7mm Kinoptic Tegea (fixed focus) T2.3	13	39
XL2	5.9mm Angenieux (fixed focus) T2	13	39
XL3	8mm Zeiss Distagon T2.4	15	45
XL5	9mm Cooke Kinetal (For ST only) T2, 9″	7	21
XL6	9.5mm Zeiss High Speed T1.3	19	57
XL7	10mm Schneider, with blimp housing, for 16BL T1.8	13	39
XS407	50mm Cooke Kinetal T2	10	30

Figure 11.3b

depend on market forces and a laboratory which has a full order book or a facilities company which has all of its equipment on hire will not need to offer a reduced rate. The other side of the coin is that a discount may hide other disadvantages, for instance a production on location with a piece of faulty equipment needs prompt assistance and no discount, however large, will compensate for lack of service. The benefits of having the level of back-up the established facilities companies can provide should not be overlooked. This applies particularly to productions with distant or overseas locations where the smaller hire company is probably unable to give support when it is needed.

OWL LIGHTING PACKAGES – PRICE LIST

	PER DAY	PER WEEK	PER WEEK (20 DAYS OR MORE)
160kW			
OWL PACKAGE 1 - HMI	£2500	£10000	£7500
OWL PACKAGE 2 - INCANDESCENT	£1250	£5000	£3750
OWL PACKAGE 3 - HMI / INCANDESCENT	£1750	£7000	£5250
100kW			
OWL PACKAGE 4 - HMI	£1900	£7600	£5700
OWL PACKAGE 5 - INCANDESCENT	£950	£3800	£2850
OWL PACKAGE 6 - HMI / INCANDESCENT	£1400	£5600	£4200
60kW			
OWL PACKAGE 7 - HMI	£1350	£5400	£4050
OWL PACKAGE 8 - INCANDESCENT	£600	£2400	£1800
OWL PACKAGE 9 - HMI / INCANDESCENT	£1050	£4200	£3150
40kW			
OWL PACKAGE 10 - HMI	£1200	£4800	£3600
OWL PACKAGE 11 - INCANDESCENT	£500	£2000	£1500
OWL PACKAGE 12 - HMI / INCANDESCENT	£850	£3400	£2550
25kW			
OWL PACKAGE 13 - HMI	£750	£3000	£2250
OWL PACKAGE 14 - INCANDESCENT	£380	£1520	£1140
OWL PACKAGE 15 - HMI / INCANDESCENT	£600	£2400	£1800

■ **Interchange of equipment kilowatt for kilowatt is possible.**

■ **Generator fuel at cost.**

■ **Mileage at 55 pence per mile per vehicle.**

■ **All prices are negotiable.**

The attention of customers is drawn to the fact that Michael Samuelson Lighting Ltd supplies equipment, materials and services only in accordance with its Conditions of Business. Copies of these Conditions of Business, which include clauses that exclude or limit the liability of the company and provide for an indemnity from the customer in certain circumstances, are available on request.

Registered in England, Company Number 1226487
Registered Office: Dudden Hill Lane, London NW10 1DS.

Figure 11.3c

Once the basic quotes have been gathered they can be related to the schedule to produce an initial budget. This first draft should be as accurate as possible within certain limits because, like the feature budget, it need only be calculated to the nearest ten or fifty units. Therefore a draft budget will look something like Figure 11.4.

There are a number of points to note about these budgets. The first line under the budget heading defines the basic parameters of the pro-

WILCOX DOLLY

O.A.L.	179.0cm	70.5"
O.A.W.	106.6cm	42.0"
O.A.H.	57.1cm	22.5"
Weight	153.7kg	350.0lbs
Wheel base	142.2cm	65.0"

Push/pull bar at rear.
Car type steering wheel and hand brake.

SUPER JIB PLATFORM

O.A.L.	68.0cm
O.A.W.	47.0cm
O.A.H.	27.0cm
Weight	

PANTHER WITH SUPER-JIB

O.A.L.	137.0cm
O.A.W.	68.0cm
O.A.H.	57.0cm
Weight	

PANTHER

Transport length	74.0cm	29.1"
Transport width	68.0cm	26.8"
Transport height	71.0cm	28.0"
Transport weight	118.0kg	260.0lbs
Maximum payload using column drive	250.0kg	550.0lbs
Maximum payload using column retracted	800.0kg	1760.0lbs
Maximum operating width	62.0cm	24.4"
Minimum tracking clearance	36.0cm	14.1"
Four-way tracking symmetry		
Maximum lens elevation (using Arri 35 BL on Sachtler Studio Head)	190.0cm	74.8"
Minimum lens clearance (using Arri 35 BL on Sachtler head and offset Adaptor)	101.0cm	39.7"
Minimum lens clearance (using Arri 35 BL on Sachtler head and low offset Adaptor)		
Column range	70.0cm	27.5"
Fastest time through column range, up and down	4.5 secs.	

Corrosion-proof, maintenance-free system.
Program stores up to 5 drive sequences, continuously variable speeds.
Integrated battery maintains program memory.
State-of-the-art electronics with automatic diagnostic routine display.
Modular quick-change circuit cards.
Kombi-wheels for track on floor use with kick-switch for curved track.

Input voltage tolerance	18-28V
Maximum power consumption	24A
Battery unit specifications	24V 9,5Ah
Charge cycle - standard charger	10 hours
Charge cycle - charge/ballast unit	5 hours

Maximum lens elevation		
(using Arri 35 BL on Sachtler Studio Head and 50cm Bazooka)	300.0cm	118.1"
Minimum lens clearance		
(using Arri 35 BL on Sachtler head, offset adaptor and Bazooka)	45.0cm	17.7"
Lift range	140.0cm	55.1"

PANTHER ACCESS

4 platforms in case	78 x 24 x 37cm
Battery and charger	54 x 18 x 38cm
2 seats, tracking bar and hand control	88 x 43 x 27cm

1.5

Figure 11.3d

duction. The draft budget for *The Dismal Science* is for a series and consequently, in documentary terms, it looks very large. However, when the figure is divided by the number of planned programmes the average is more acceptable. Because it is planned to be shot on video the stock cost is relatively low and the editing cost is proportionately high when compared with the film budget for *The Green and the Gold*. This latter budget is for a programme planned to be filmed in Ireland and as such the travel

```
DRAFT BUDGET            THE DISMAL SCIENCE            DATE:

This budget is based on a 9 week studio shoot on video.

A Story and script                               £     400
B Producer's fee              30 weeks @ 460      £  13800
  Director's fee                                  £  13800
  Writer's fee                                    £  18000
─────────────────────────────────────────────────────────
SUBTOTAL                                          £  46000
─────────────────────────────────────────────────────────
C Salaries: Production (pm.pa.re)   840 X 30w     £  25200
            Crew                   2500 X  9w      £  22500
            Editing                 600 X 25w      £  15000
            Additional              800 X 10w      £   8000
D Art department                                  £   6000
E Artistes; cast               600 X 6 X 2        £   7200
F Music; direction, musicians                     £   3000
G Costumes and wigs                               £   3000
H Misc. production stores                         £   1200
I Video stock                  Ratio @ 6 to 1     £   2000
  Laboratory charges                              £   9000
J Studio                                          £   6000
  Editing: Off-line            400 X 24w          £   9600
           On-line                 X  2w          £  11000
K Equipment                   1500 X  9w          £  13500
L Power                                           £    700
M Travel & transport: Location                    £   6000
                      Studio                      £   1000
N Hotel & living expenses; location              £   9600
O Insurances                                      £   3600
P PAYE/SIC                                         £  21000
Q Publicity salaries & expenses                   £    800
R Miscellaneous expenses                          £   1200
S Sets & models: Construction                     £   1800
                 Props/dressing                   £   1000
U Location facilities                             £    500
─────────────────────────────────────────────────────────
SUBTOTAL                                          £ 189400
─────────────────────────────────────────────────────────
Y Finance & legal                                 £   1000
Z Overheads                                       £   3600
─────────────────────────────────────────────────────────
SUBTOTAL                                          £   4600
─────────────────────────────────────────────────────────
TOTAL                                             £ 240000

Average price per programme                       £  40000
```

Figure 11.4a

```
BUDGET SUMMARY          THE  GREEN  AND  THE  GOLD        DATE:

Budget based on a 3 week shoot and an 8 week editing period.

A Story and script                                      £    1000
  Development fee                                        £     100
B Producer's fee                                         £    3600
  Director's fee                                         £    3600

Subtotal                                                 £    8300

C Salaries:  Production                                  £    3300
             Crew                                        £    3000
             Editing                                     £    4800
             Additional                                  £     600
D Art department (graphics)                              £     300
E Artistes appearance fee                                £     200
F Music; direction, musicians                            £     500
H Misc. production stores                                £     200
I Film stock              Ratio @ 10/1 on 16 mm          £    1500
  Laboratory charges                                     £    4400
J Studio/editing rentals                                 £    1000
K Equipment                                              £    2500
L Power                                                  £     100
M Travel & transport: Location                           £    4400
                      Studio                             £     300
N Hotel & living expenses: Location                      £    3200
                           Studio                        £     400
O Insurances                                             £    1300
P PAYE/Hol. Cred.                                        £    5000
R Miscellaneous expenses                                 £     300
U Location facilities                                    £     400

Subtotal                                                 £   37700

Y Finance & legal                                        £     400
Z Overheads                                              £    2600

Subtotal                                                 £    3000

TOTAL                                                    £   49000
```

Figure 11.4b

4	CHANNEL FOUR PROGRAMME BUDGET	SCHEDULE 4
Schedule Reference:	Direct Costs and Overheads	Total £
5	Story/Scripts/Development	
6	Producer/Director	
7	Artists	
8	Presenters/Interviewees etc	
9	Production Unit Salaries	
10	Assistant Directors/Continuity	
11	Crew – Camera	
12	Crew – Sound	
13	Crew – Lighting	
14	Crew – Art Department	
15	Crew – Wardrobe/Make-Up/Hair	
16	Crew – Editing	
17	Crew – Second Unit	
18	Salary & Wage Related Overheads	
19	Materials – Art Department	
20	Materials – Wardrobe/Make-Up/Hair	
21	Production Equipment	
22	Facility Package Arrangements	
23	Studios/Outside Broadcast	
24	Other Production Facilities	
25	Film/Tape Stock	
26	Picture/Sound Post-Production – Film	
27	Picture/Sound Post-Production – Tape	
28	Archive Material	
29	Rostrum/Graphics	
30	Music (Copyright/Performance)	
31	Travel/Transport	
32	Hotel/Living	
33	Other Production Costs	
34	Insurance/Finance/Legal	
35	Production Overheads	
36	Theatrical Performances	
37	Continuation Sheets	
38		
39		
40		
	TOTAL DIRECT COSTS AND OVERHEADS £	

Figure 11.5

Channel 4 Programme Budget
Page 4

and transport and the hotel and living expenses for the location shooting are proportionately much higher than those figures for the series.

Figure 11.5 is an example of a budget summary as produced by a television company for its own budget form. Every documentary budget will depend on the style of programme being planned and the above budgets should only be taken as examples of how the costing of a programme might be arrived at. The refining process will continue as the

CHANNEL FOUR PROGRAMME COST REPORT

PROGRAMME TITLE: _____

PROGRAMME NUMBER: _____

COST REPORT PREPARED BY: _____

COST REPORT DATE: _____

Schedule Reference		A. Total Spent per Cash Book £	B. Creditors £	C. Total Cost to Date (A + B) £	D. Costs to Completion £	E. Estimated Final Cost (C + D) £	F. Budget as Agreed by C4 £	G. (Under)/Over Budget (E – F) £
5	Story/Scripts/Development							
6	Producer/Director							
7	Artists							
8	Presenters/Interviewers etc							
9	Production Unit Salaries							
10	Assistant Directors/Continuity							
11	Crew – Camera							
12	Crew – Sound							
13	Crew – Lighting							
14	Crew – Art Department							
15	Crew – Wardrobe/Make-Up/Hair							
16	Crew – Editing							
17	Crew – Second Unit							
18	Salary & Wage Related Overheads							
19	Materials – Art Department							
20	Materials – Wardrobe/Make-Up/Hair							
21	Production Equipment							
22	Facility Package Arrangements							
23	Studios/Outside Broadcast							
24	Other Production Facilities							
25	Film/Tape Stock							
26	Picture/Sound Post Production – Film							
27	Picture/Sound Post Production – Tape							
28	Archive Material							
29	Rostrum/Graphics							
30	Music (Copyright/Performance)							
31	Travel/Transport							
32	Hotel/Living							
33	Other Production Costs							
34	Insurance/Finance/Legal							
35	Production Overheads							
36	Theatrical Performances							
37	Continuation Sheets							
38								
39								
40								
	TOTAL DIRECT COSTS AND OVERHEADS	£	£	£	£	£	£	£
	PRODUCTION FEE							
	CONTINGENCIES							
	COMPLETION GUARANTEE							
	TOTAL	£	£	£	£	£	£	£

RECONCILIATION

FUNDING

Cash Advances – C4

– Other (specify)

Deposit a/c interest

Creditors (Column B)

VAT Due to Customs & Excise

Suspense Accounts (specify)

TOTAL   I £ _____

USE OF FUNDS

Total Cost to Date (Column C)

Bank Balances (per bank reconciliations)

Petty Cash

Debtors – floats (attach list)

– Other

Other (specify)

TOTAL   II £ _____

Note: 1. All costs and advances should be reported exclusive of VAT.
2. Totals I and II must balance.

Channel 4 Programme Cost Report
Page 1

Figure 11.6

production progresses, particularly with service companies who may be prepared to offer discounts or other deals depending on whether they see a benefit in working with your production.

The calculation of the budget is a vital stage in a production and one in which the production manager must be involved. Only by fully understanding how the costings were put together can the finances of a project be followed and controlled. It is for this reason that companies which commission independent productions, particularly television companies, want to be involved in the budgeting process. This should be welcomed by any programme maker because getting the budget right is a major step towards getting the production right. Figure 11.6 shows an example of a television programme cost report.

Having got the right budget, the next important financial action is to keep it under control.

CHAPTER 12

CONTROLLING THE BUDGET

Annual income twenty pounds, annual expenditure nineteen pounds, result happiness. Annual income twenty pounds, annual expenditure twenty-one pounds, result misery.

W.C. Fields as Mr Micawber in David Copperfield

Mr Micawber's dictum in George Cukor's film of *David Copperfield* applies to the production manager more than most people on a film because controlling the budget is one of the key jobs for which he or she will be responsible.

Budget control is a function which takes place before, during and after the shoot and is vital if a production is to meet its contract requirements. It is important because the contract will almost certainly allow the financiers or completion guarantors to take over the film if they are unhappy with an over-run.

Having spent a lot of time and effort to set up a production it is stupid to lose the film because of insufficient control on production expenditure. It may be thought that the easiest way to avoid having a completion guarantor called in to finish the film is not to have the completion of the film guaranteed. This is not usually possible as most financiers will not even consider funding an independent production without a completion guarantee. If this seems unreasonable it should be remembered that there is a plus side to the equation, which is that completion guarantors do not wish to be called in either. Therefore, once they have agreed to act as guarantors, they will be doing their best to help the film arrive on budget. This often means that they will help the producer to calculate a correct budget in the first place.

On a production made for television the backers will have a similar control over the finance. Because the budget will probably not be large enough for a completion guarantor to be involved the financiers will call on the production fee to make up the balance. When a contract for a programme is signed by an independent production company the sponsoring company usually agrees to pay a production fee which is calculated as a percentage of the budget. This is paid to the production company for the making of the film and is recognized as the production company's profit.

If the production goes over the budget then the extra money is initially found from this production fee. However, if the film costs more than the budget and the production fee, then the producer will have to face some real problems and, as indicated above, may lose control of the production because the sponsoring company may well decide to act and have it taken over by some other producer or company, if not by themselves. Consequently it is better to face the cost implications before this position is arrived at.

Clearly it is of no benefit for a production to go over budget, so the question to be considered is how can the budget be controlled? What mechanisms can be used so that the people responsible for the film are aware of the financial progress of the production?

The first method used is the cash flow forecast. This is a 'tool' which is essential for the running of any business and is a vital one for controlling the budget of a film. One of the roles of the producer, production manager or production accountant will be the calculation of a cash flow forecast.

A cash flow forecast is essentially what it says. A business produces a forecast of how the money in the business is to be earned and spent; in other words how the cash will flow. On a film the way the money is 'earned' is usually defined in the contract. It generally comes in tranches or blocks on money. The first tranche is delivered on signature of the contract, the second on the commencement of principal photography and the third on completion of principal photography. On a television series there may well be additional tranches with each episode.

This is the expected formula for financing a production but individual contracts may vary the times when the money is handed over to the production company. The size of these tranches is usually arrived at by seeing how the money for the production is planned to be used and this is shown in the cash flow forecast.

Thus a simple cash flow for an item in a documentary may look something like the following:

PRE-PRODUCTION				SHOOT		POST-PRODUCTION					
Week: 1	2	3	4	5	6	7	8	9	10	11	12
Item: £5	£5	£10	£10	£20	£20	£15	£10	£5	£5	£5	£10

In this example the budgeted item costs £120 and the production period is 12 weeks.

Obviously a very basic cash flow of £10 per week could be planned but it would be unusual for an item to have a cash flow of this simplicity. Therefore it is more likely for the cash flow to have highs and lows in it, as in the example above.

It can be seen that, for the item under consideration in this cash flow, the period of highest expected expenditure is during the shoot. It should be realized that the period of high expenditure, if there is one, depends on the budget item. Thus a cutting room would have no expenditure in weeks 1, 2, 3, and 4 but would expect to have a constant expenditure from week 5 to the end of the production. However, the expenditure for camera hire would be expected only to cover the shooting period. The production office will expect to have a steady cash flow throughout the making of the programme but these expenses may be on a monthly basis rather a weekly one. The laboratory costs will fluctuate depending on which stage the picture is at.

Therefore, from the above example, the figures needed to decide how the financing of the contract will be drawn up are £30 for the pre-production period, £40 for the shooting period and £50 for the post-production period.

As mentioned in Chapter 10, the budget summary at the beginning of many budget forms is a basic form of cash flow but if proper control is to be maintained a more detailed cash flow will be required. As ever, the more information the better or, in this instance, the more detailed the cash flow the better. It is from the information provided by the cash flow that the production manager is able to keep control of the costs.

Although cash flow may be calculated on a monthly basis for the pre- and post-production phases of the production during the shoot, which is the time of highest expenditure, it should be calculated more closely, at least for weekly expenditure.

The cash flow forecast gives the producer, the accountant and the production office a tool by which the actual cost of the production can be measured.

As with any other management practice the business of checking on the progress of expenditure is essentially quite simple; the difficult action is deciding what to do when things, start to go wrong.

The first need, however, is to understand how to keep a check on the budget and this is done by regularly completing a weekly or monthly cost statement. Only on a documentary shoot would a monthly return be acceptable. A feature film's costs need to be checked on a weekly basis. The cost statement is usually made up as follows:

	A	B	C	B+C	D	D-(B+C)
Budget Item	Cost for period	Accumulated cost to date	Estimated cost to complete	Final cost	Budget	(Over)/ Under

This refers to a particular section from the budget form which is under consideration like art department or equipment hire. The headings are as follows.

Cost for period: This is the money that has been spent during a specified time. The period can be of any length but the longer it is the less control can be kept over spending. Therefore a month should be the maximum and a week is the usual length of time considered during the shooting period and for the whole production of a feature. In fact, completion guarantors generally demand weekly cost reports as part of their contract.

Accumulated cost to date: This is the actual expenditure at the date of the cost report. This includes the cost for the previous period.

Estimated cost to complete: This is the estimated amount of money needed to complete the production from the date of the cost report. This figure should be arrived at by adding together the estimated cost of the remaining weeks of the production, these figures having been extracted from the cash flow for the production. This is the reason why a detailed cash flow forecast has to be calculated because this forecast charts the estimated amount of money required by the production at the time when the cost statement is being prepared. Therefore, from the example cash flow on page 100, the cost to complete figure after the first week will be £115, after week 6 it will be £50 and after week 11 it will be £10.

Final cost: This is the sum of the cost to date and the cost to complete.

Budget: This is the figure in the agreed budget.

(Over)/Under: This is the difference between the cost to complete and the budget and it gives an indication of how the finances of the production are proceeding. If the cost to complete is greater than the budget then the budget item is running over; if it is less than the budget the budget item is running under.

Thus, taking part of the budget from the example in Chapter 10, a budget analysis for cost control would look something like the following. (In this example the cost period is a week, the total shooting period is 10 weeks, the production is in its third week of filming, the studio part of the shoot begins in the fifth week and the total production time is 52 weeks.)

The final figures in the (Under)/Over column need to be looked at closely, particularly any item which is wide of the predicted budget, be it too high on over spend or too low on underspend. It must be realized that any figure that is too far from the original estimate should be a real cause for concern and the reason for the initial mis-evaluation, high or low, must be established as soon as possible. The worst possible reason is a badly calculated budget, although with the amount of advice and assistance given for a feature and the extent of help and expertise provided by finance directors and cost controllers in television companies this should not happen.

If the costs on a production are running over budget it is obvious that the reason has to be discovered promptly so that corrective action may be taken.

Budget item	Accum cost for period	Cost to date	Cost to complete	Final cost	Budget	(Under) /Over
M. Travel & transport:						
Location	4412	18 545	43 000	61 545	60 000	1545
Studio	1051	4271	14 000	18 271	19 000	(729)
N. Hotel & living expenses:						
Location	37 067	59 210	100 600	159 810	159 600	210
Studio	0	0	5500	5500	5500	0

Looking at the example above, both the location items have gone over budget. However, the first is a much more serious over-run than the second because, in terms of the total budget item, the first is 2.57% over budget whereas the second is only 0.13% over budget. Also, there is less room to claw back the over-run.

The first studio item has a small saving. The producer, production manager and production accountant should be aware of the actual situation in terms of losses and savings but, as a broad guideline, the director should only be told of an overspending because, generally speaking, a director who is told of a saving will immediately want to spend it three times over, so it is better never to tell the director if the production is in the black.

The final item in the example simply shows that the production has not yet reached this part of the budget.

Although a monthly cost report may be acceptable in the pre- and post-production phases, during the shoot, which is the time of highest expenditure, the cost reports should be as frequent as possible so that any overspend can be corrected as soon as possible. In this respect the advantages of computer-programmed budgets should be realized. These programs can provide quick, accurate and up-to-date reports on expenditure, besides keeping track of all sorts of information useful for cost control, such as which items have been hired for the film and which have been purchased. The fact that a daily costing can be given means that proper financial control can be exerted over the production and this is true for every production regardless of size. Feature films, because of their complexity, need the help that computers can offer in keeping track of all the different areas in the production while small productions, because of their minimal staffs, benefit from the time saving that computers can provide.

On a feature shoot the accounting is usually the direct responsibility of the production accountant and if the film begins to run over budget then the producer is the person who has to be told as he or she is responsible for raising the finance to cover the shortfall. It should be realized that a shortfall may not be the result of an uncontrolled shoot but can occur for a number of reasons, for example, where a film has two or more backers and one of them pulls out at the last minute or during the shoot. This is not a common situation but it has happened and obviously there is no definitive answer on what may be the best policy for the producer to follow.

However, under these circumstances the production office should let the unit know what the situation is, particularly if it affects their immediate work. Taking the crew into the production's confidence is good basic management because a crew which does not know the position will hear lots of rumours and under these conditions it will not work well. In fact it will almost certainly be considering if it should be working at all particularly if it believes it is not going to be paid beyond the two weeks' salary which the production is obliged to hold in escrow.

The reasons for overspend are numerous but some parts of a budget are more vulnerable than others. In the standard budget form in Chapter 10 it can be seen that all the 'above the line' items (A, B and E) are agreed and fixed and, as fees are usually agreed for the total time of the production, it is unlikely that there will be a variation in this part of the budget.

The first below the line item is the production unit salaries (C). The most likely reason for an overspend in this section is the crew being asked to do overtime. A properly planned schedule and budget should account for the additional cost of early calls and night shoots, but this will not necessarily eliminate the need for additional overtime and a decision has to be made as to what is an acceptable level of overtime in return for required footage and what is not. A crew on a feature can cost between £800 and £2000 per hour, or more depending on the size of the shoot, and overtime can add 50% to this bill. On a commercial, which often will have only a 1 day schedule, it is not always possible to avoid overtime, but a feature or a documentary film, shot over a period of weeks and properly scheduled, should provide alternative times for filming and these should be considered before calling for overtime.

The factor that has to be realized is that undercrewing will not necessarily save money as it may well result in additional hirings which were not budgeted for. An example of this is best illustrated by the story of a producer who, in an effort to save money, decided to employ a single hairdresser on his production. The hairdresser had asked for a full-time assistant but this request was refused on grounds of cost; a request for an assistant to be employed as necessary was also refused for the same reason. Eventually there came a morning when the three principal artistes were required on the same day and each required an hour with the hairdresser, with the result that the crew stood around for a couple of hours waiting for the hairdresser to finish his work with the cast. This was clearly not the most efficient way of using time, particularly as the cost of paying the crew to stand around would have paid for a full-time assistant hairdresser for a couple of weeks. This is why it is important to understand the real cost of running a crew.

The next three items in the budget, art department, artistes, and musical direction and music (D, E and F) fall into the same category as the production unit. People need time to do their jobs and those who know best how much time they need are the technicians, artistes, actors and musicians themselves, so their advice should be sought and listened to. A production manager would not expect the crew employed during the pre- and post-production periods, like art department staff or editors, to be working lots of overtime. On the other hand, during the shoot the cast, stand-ins, doubles, stunt crew and crowd, when they are used, will all essentially be running on the same schedule as the shooting crew.

Here again, particularly with crowds, the question of value for money has to be considered. It may be more expensive to ask for 300 crowd artists to return the next day than to run into a couple of hours overtime because, as with much of film production, it is not just the simple cost of the artiste's fee that has to be considered – there are all the other related matters involved in the shoot. Three-hundred extras called for a second day means that catering and transport for the personnel has to be again provided. It does not need higher mathematics to realize that 300 lunches at £5 a head, or £1500, is well on the way to 2 hours' overtime for the production unit, and the extras.

Musicians are booked in blocks of time known as 'sessions' and the music director/composer should be closely consulted about how much time is needed for the recording of the music.

Costumes and wigs (G) should be easily controlled but the next item, miscellaneous production stores (H), can cause havoc, not so much on a feature film but certainly on a documentary where a small sum spent is a larger percentage of the budget. Granted that a roll of camera tape is not in itself an expensive item but it can become so if a clapper loader or camera assistant decides that every tin of film needs to be wrapped in its own roll of camera tape.

Budget control begins with the small things and an example of this is the difference between first- and second-class postage which is some 30%, 6p may be insignificant in terms of the total budget but 30% on the total of that budget is highly significant.

Film stock and laboratory charges (I) is another area where money can be wasted unless proper thought is given to what exactly is required for the successful completion of the production. The camera person who does not realize that short ends, if properly looked after, can be sold on at the end of the shoot, or the editor who assumes that additional prints can be ordered thoughtlessly, need to be educated not to squander resources, although it should be said that most competent technicians are aware of budget constraints and do not waste the production company's money.

The cost of studio rentals, equipment and power (J, K and L) all ultimately depend on the length of the shoot but the budget may be under pressure from the outset if the items hired are not used. It is a rare camera technician or sound recordist who does not feel that every item in the catalogue might not be needed during filming. Therefore budget control begins at the planning stage and a production manager should be convinced that the equipment hired is going to be used, otherwise it is a waste of money.

One of the areas most frequently underbudgeted and hardest to keep under control is travel and transport (M). For example, items that need to be collected and delivered fall into this area of the budget and the temptation to call for a dispatch rider whenever something has to be sent promptly means that the cost of the method is not being considered, and even if it is the production's own transport doing the delivery this is still a cost to the production. The average travelling salesman is only too aware of the expense of casual mileage done in the process of business, in terms of time and petrol, and knows that the cost soon builds up. This is equally true for the running around needed during filming, so it is not the long distances which are hard to calculate but the short trips here, there and everywhere which eventually bite into the budget.

Hotel and living expenses (N) is, more often than not, another area of high expense unless due care is taken. Firstly, this means finding out and comparing the prices for all the accommodation near the location. In the United Kingdom the cost of a room in one establishment can sometimes be double that of a similar room in another establishment in the same area, and overseas locations can present even wider price ranges. The important point is to be sure that the accommodation is of a level that is acceptable and beneficial to the unit; cheap, uncomfortable, noisy hotels do not let the crew get the rest it needs after a hard day's work and this can hardly benefit the film.

With regard to that part of this item covering expenses, there are clear guidelines in the agreements on what is allowable and the important point here is to ensure that the members of the unit know in advance what expenses the production will accept. This point should preferably be agreed at the time contracts are signed.

The insurance and social security items (O and P) should be fairly straightforward although the latter will be affected by overtime payments.

Publicity salaries and expenses (Q) has the possible variable of expenses in the item. There are enough stories in the business and entertainment world about the abuse of expenses to alert a production manager to the need to monitor this item closely.

The majority of the miscellaneous expenses (R) are for set fees but, like the above item, there is still room for money to be wasted if careful control is not maintained. Any expense which does not directly contribute to the final film should be closely questioned.

Of the final items in the budget two of these, sets and models, and special effects (S and T), can have enormous cost spirals if they are not properly planned. Part of proper planning essentially involves having a clear idea of what is wanted and keeping to it. A production becomes expensive when the director asks for something which was not planned for. An example of this is an occasion when the Oscar-winning cameraman David Watkin was working on Franco Zeffirelli's film *La Traviata*.

A particular scene had been agreed the night before but in the morning, after it had been lit, Zeffirelli decided he wanted it to be lit by candles. Instant chaos! The production office rushed out to buy hundreds of candles, the labourers on the set began to place and light the candles, the schedule for the morning was thrown aside. Eventually, at about lunchtime, the set was ready and Zeffirelli was asked to approve it. His reaction was to shout, asking who had had the stupid idea of lighting the scene by candles and ordering the set to be cleared immediately. Zeffirelli then went to lunch and filming began in the afternoon with the original lighting set-up. An expensive morning for little or no return and clearly not something that can be done too often if the production is to maintain its schedule and consequently its budget.

This factor becomes even more important the shorter the shooting time: the loss of a morning on a 3 week schedule is 3.33% of the filming time; the same loss on a 12 week schedule is 0.83% of the filming time. This is not to say that there should never be times when the director is allowed to explore the artistic possibilities of a particular scene, because film making is a creative process, but it is also an expensive process and a production manager needs to be aware of the cost repercussions resulting from any action taken by any member of the crew.

The other side of the equation in the cash flow forecast is the income that is received by the production. Once the backers have agreed the budget they will want to know when the production needs the money and how much in each instance; certainly no financier will give the total budget to the production on commencement of the pre-production phase. As mentioned before, the model scheme for financing a film is to provide a third on signature of the contract, a third on commencement of principal photography and a third on completion of the shooting phase. However, this model can be altered to suit the individual backer and is open to negotiation on every production. For example, the financing of independent productions for Channel 4 television is usually agreed on the basis of specific sums being paid at particular points in the production in accordance with the cash flow that has been calculated with the company's finance directors, the cash flow being 'schedule four' in their budget form.

The second point that must be remembered regarding the funding of a film is that the second and subsequent tranches of money are usually not paid until the money provided to date has been accounted for by the production. Again, independent productions working with Channel 4 are required to complete a 'programme cost report' which has to reconcile the monies advanced against monies spent, owing or in the bank, and these figures have to balance. This essentially is the 'cost statement' outlined above. Only when the balance is approved will the next tranche of finance be given to the production – hence the real need to keep up-to-date accounts for prompt presentation.

A final point, which cannot be stressed enough, is the need to keep all the documentation. On those occasions when a production goes badly wrong and legal action is taken, this documentation will be wanted as evidence of the way the production was managed, and as such will gain legal status in any lawsuit. Certainly the backers and the completion guarantors will want copies as will anyone else who is directly involved with the production, so none of this information should be disposed of until long after the programme is finished and no longer has a commercial life.

Three things must be remembered regarding the financial control of a production. Firstly, time is money and sticking to the schedule is a major key in keeping control over the budget. Secondly, the keeping of up-to-date accounts is vital if the actual financial situation is to be known accurately. Thirdly, prompt action must be taken once the budget is seen to be going astray. It will not correct itself and so cannot afford to be left. These points will not guarantee that a production will stay on budget but they will help an understanding of the position if something does start to go wrong.

CHAPTER 13

INITIAL PREPARATION FOR THE SHOOT

The majority of the previous chapters in this book are concerned with the preparation for a shoot. The script is the first step in preparing for a feature, the proposal is the first step for a documentary. The processes of breaking down, budgeting and scheduling are all essential steps in the pre-production phase of any film, regardless of size or complexity.

However, depending on the individual project, there are a number of other requirements which need to be completed if a production is to progress smoothly. These activities cover a range of subjects and will vary from production to production. Clearly there will be different needs for a feature film shot in Britain against a documentary filmed in Africa.

The problems of casting, crewing, equipment hire, location finding, insurances, terms of engagement and relations with the unions will all vary from film to film.

With the vast number of things that have to be done on a production the question is which should be dealt with first? As ever, part of the answer to this question depends on the needs of the production. Part of the production manager's evaluation of a project will include an appraisal of what needs to be done in what order. A cutting room does not need to be hired at the beginning of pre-production, and detailed insurance, a vital necessity, sometimes cannot be completed until it is known precisely what has to be covered, although certain insurances have to be dealt with up front. Therefore these things can be left for later in the pre-production phase. On the other hand, a documentary which has a requirement to interview particular people cannot proceed until the production is sure that they are available. Equally this may apply on a drama where the director has specific actors in mind. Until their availability is confirmed time may well be wasted arranging for them to be insured.

The following sections are those areas which should be considered first when preparing for a shoot.

FINDING THE CAST OR INTERVIEWEE

On a feature film, casting is the business of the casting director and, if no one has been recommended, it is a case of looking through the industry directories. Initially this may be for names but it may also be for agencies who look after artistes and performers. If the budget does not stretch to a casting director then someone in the production office has to be responsible for casting. Although the director or producer may do the choosing, a production assistant will certainly have to do the chasing and the standard contracts. The usual starting point is *Spotlight* which is a very comprehensive directory of Equity members. Once the process is begun leads will open up but the work cannot be started soon enough, because one does not have to be looking for a 'Scarlett O'Hara' to have problems with casting.

The casting of children presents additional problems. Firstly, twenty-eight days' notice is required to obtain a licence for children under sixteen. Secondly, they have to be chaperoned, with a minimum of one chaperone to every four children, although in practice this usually means two, so that more than the performers have to be dealt with when children are on a shoot. Thirdly they are only allowed to work for restricted hours. It is one of the chaperone's duties to ensure that the proper hours are worked and therefore this fact must be taken into consideration when planning the schedule. Finally the Local Education Authority may wish to visit the shoot to check on the working conditions of the children and, depending on the circumstances, the production may have to provide schooling facilities for the children if they are involved on the production over a long period.

In the case of crowd artists the FAA should be approached if the filming takes place within 40 miles of Charing Cross, London, but outside this area extras can be hired from the local population. For this, an advertisement in the local paper or enquiries at any nearby repertory theatre or company are two ways to start; amateur drama groups and the local labour exchange are other options. However, even on distant locations a production manager is obliged to take FAA members if they are suitable and on site at their own expense.

With regard to documentaries, the need to find people to be interviewed is usually the job of the researcher and good researchers know what routes to follow. Again, this work cannot start soon enough because, unlike professional performers, the interviewees may not be available at times convenient to the production, so either the schedule has to be changed or alternative interviewees have to be found. Although neither casting nor research is the direct concern of a production manager they, like all the work done on a production, need help from the production office and so it is the job of a production manager to provide the resources and back-up so that the work can be done effectively. Also, the production manager is responsible for making sure that the various departments are doing their work and that it is up to schedule and within budget.

CREW HIRE

The crewing of a film is the business of the production manager although individual directors or producers may have preferences for technicians they have worked with before and the lighting camera person will usually want to work with a crew they already know.

This is equally true for the sound, editorial and technical disciplines on a production, so the process of finding a crew is often determined from the moment the producer, director and possibly the production manager are appointed. Something which needs to be kept in mind in the choosing of the crew relates to the productions where major stars are involved. Some stars come with 'an entourage'. Often, the bigger the star the bigger the entourage and this means that you hire who they want or you do not get them.

However, stars excluded, if the instigators of the production do not have particular personnel in mind, then they can be found by referring to trade directories or the technicians' own agents. Many key personnel like performers have their own agents. On all productions, but particularly on a low-budget production one of the best ways of finding out who might be available is to refer to the film technicians' own union which runs a crew agency service called 'CREWS'. There are also commercial crewing agencies, and these can be found in the trade directories, as can specialist agencies which cater for specific disciplines such as make-up or hair-dressing.

LOCATIONS

With the decrease in size and general improvement of equipment more and more productions follow the option of filming on location. A location is any place which is not part of a recognized studio. However, some studios have such a good relationship with their locality that they can offer facilities otherwise not available on the lot. Shepperton, for example, has a church near at hand which has often been used in films, thanks mainly to the managers of the studio.

Broadly speaking locations can be divided into overseas, at home (home being the country of the production), resident, and daily travel locations. They can further be divided into public or private properties.

Public or private, a production will need to gain permission from someone to shoot on the location. The location finder or location manager will know how best to get these permissions but for a documentary or low-budget production the researcher or production assistant probably will be appointed to this task.

Public locations, such as streets or parks, will need the permission of the police (Figure 13.1 shows police guidance notes), and/or the local authority. The time taken to get this permission varies from place to place and also depends on the location in question and the complexity

No. 833

METROPOLITAN POLICE

FILMING IN STREETS

The following notes are issued for the information and guidance of persons undertaking filming in the streets and public places:-

(1) Nothing in the nature of a staged crime or street disturbance will be permitted.

(2) No filming can be permitted which would interfere with the operation of the parking meter schemes or give rise to any contravention of Road Traffic Acts or Regulations.

(3) Any filming must be undertaken on the sole responsibility of the promoters and participants, and no facilities can be granted by Police.

(4) The Commissioner of Police has no power to authorize the use of streets for the purposes of filming and does not issue permits purporting to do so, but police will not normally object to proposed filming provided that:-

(a) No obstruction or annoyance is caused and the directions of police on duty are observed.

(b) In the event of complaints being made or annoyance being caused filming ceases immediately at the request of Police.

(c) Where artificial lighting is used care must be taken to ensure that no obstruction or danger is caused by cables, wires, etc., and no danger or annoyance is caused by dazzle from the lights.

(d) As far as possible filming is arranged to take place when traffic, both vehicular and pedestrian, is lightest, e.g., on a Sunday morning.

(e) When it is proposed to film actors dressed in police uniforms, rehearsals are to be carried out in plain clothes. The fitting of gongs, bells, two-tone horns and blue flashing lights to pseudo-police vehicles is prohibited by law.

(f) Any special requirements of police about a particular filming are observed.

M.P.72(E)

Figure 13.1

of the shoot. Motorways, for example, can be filmed on but a lot of careful negotiation has to take place with the police before they will grant permission. Wherever the production is filming some permission will be needed and it is far better to get it before the unit arrives rather than have lengthy discussions with the park keeper, game warden or other official at a time when the crew could and should be working. It also obviates the likelihood of being obliged to pay outrageous fees in order to remain on the location.

OVERSEAS LOCATIONS

All the problems which apply to locations at home also apply to overseas locations but there are a number of additional factors to be considered when a production goes overseas. The first factor is the problem of getting into the country in question.

The straightforward answer to this question is to get in touch with the embassy or consulate of the country to be visited and find out if there are any laws or restrictions which have to be complied with. Also, trade directories, which usually have information on the the first points of contact with individual countries, can be checked. As with most preproduction requirements this action cannot begin soon enough, particularly with Third World countries whose bureaucracies are often very slow in responding to requests for information, even requests from their own embassies.

However, this does not mean that they will be difficult to get into. Ironically the United States of America is one of the hardest countries for film crews to enter, because of its labour laws, whereas some countries, like China, are relatively easy to deal with because of their central bureaucracies, and often say simply 'yes' or 'no' and that is that. However, if the answer is 'yes', then they usually like to provide the production with a 'minder' who may or may not be a great deal of help. This is something that never happens in the USA or other democratic countries where a production may well need to find its own 'minder' who knows the local area. If a 'minder' is imposed on the unit it is generally better to try and work with them and use their knowledge rather than waste time and effort combating the local bureaucracy.

In this respect the USA is one of the most helpful countries as most of the major cities have special civic and police departments for dealing with locations and crews on location shooting. A number of states also have their own Film Commissions which have been set up to encourage productions to be made in the state in question and will often provide a lot of free advice and assistance.

Thus visas are the first essential items and at the same time some effort should be made to try to find out if any other clearances are required. Some countries expect film crews to have local press passes, while in other countries the local police expect individuals to carry identity papers, over and above a passport, and certainly a union card has fulfilled this role in the past. So, once the production knows it is going to a particular country then the more information about the country that can be gleaned the better.

There are few countries which film crews have not visited and through the union or other contacts technicians can be found who can give advice on the problems that may be encountered. There are local crews who can be consulted and employed. This latter consideration should not be dismissed out of hand even if the unit is going to a Third World country, because it should be remembered that to fly to South America or South East Asia may cost in the region of £1500 per crew member and a local electrician, interpreter, production assistant or any other non-technical crew member will almost certainly not cost as much in terms of salary and yet may also provide a quantity of invaluable local information. The saving here may considerably offset their inexperience of working with UK film technicians.

Part of the purpose of obtaining information about the country to be visited is to learn about local laws and customs so that everyone can be made aware of what is expected before arrival.

The one person who should be able to help with any local problems is the British Consul, so he or she should be contacted as soon as the unit arrives, for there is little the Consul can do until he or she is aware of your presence yet much help may be offered once contact has been made, particularly with productions which may be regarded as politically sensitive by the host country. Although helpful on a political level, the Embassy or Consulate sometimes is not so helpful on a practical level. Therefore, contact with a local freight agent will often produce a quicker and more efficient result, as invariably they can tell you exactly what is required to clear goods through customs.

It is impossible to say what particular problems may be presented by any one country, so clearly it is up to the production office, usually through the researcher, to find out. However, there are a wide range of requirements which governments can impose and, for example, these may include any of the following restrictions:

Currency demands and laws: Some countries insist that a certain sum of their currency is bought before entry is allowed; other countries have strict controls on the import or export of their money.

Bond demands: Where the value, or part of the value, of the unit's equipment has to be lodged with the local government to guarantee that the equipment is not sold in that country.

Import and export restrictions: One of the reasons for hiring equipment from the larger outfits is because of their wide knowledge of the many import, export and currency problems that particular governments and their countries may present and of the ways of overcoming them. This is a clear case of where the hire money is buying more services than those provided in the simple hire of equipment.

To speed up travel abroad, the ATA carnet system was developed. The carnet is a document which is issued by the London Chamber of Commerce and Industry, and if a production is filming in or travelling through certain countries on the way to a shoot, a carnet will be required.

It takes 24 hours to process a carnet, and certain very specific conditions must be complied with if the document is to work properly. The simple purpose of the carnet is to allow goods, namely equipment, not consumables like stock, to be imported and re-exported into the listed countries without having to pay the usually required taxes and duties. Remembering that some duties are calculated as a percentage of the value of the goods being imported, it can be easily seen why the carnet is such a valuable document.

The Euro carnet is a similar system for EEC countries although these are covered by the ATA carnet.

The important point to remember when using a carnet is to follow the rules, if they are not followed or mistakes are made it can cost more in time and money than doing the job properly in the first place. This point also extends, to the possibility of needing to raise a bond to cover the goods while they are in the country. The one thing no production manager should do is to pay cash for a temporary import bond—it is very likely that the cash will never be seen again. The correct way to deal with this problem is to find a good freight agent who will be able to advise on how to process the paperwork properly and, as with the carnet, careful work and not cutting corners will always pay dividends in the long run.

Social customs: These can prove to be a minefield of troubles if they are unknowingly transgressed, the laws of alcohol in Moslem countries being the most obvious example, and it should be realized that an action taken in ignorance often does not hold much sway with the local police or court and can be very expensive to correct.

Press and censorship laws: These can vary widely from country to country and often prove to be more sensitive than any economic restrictions that may be in force.

These are some of the requirements which individual countries may impose and in order to complete a production these restrictions have to be understood, overcome or avoided. As usual, time is needed for solutions to be worked out for these problems and therefore the sooner they are discovered and recognized the better.

An important point to remember when on an overseas location is the state of the local currency in relation to the production's source of funding and with respect to local inflation. The pound and the dollar are hard currencies which can buy a lot of services in those countries with weak economies, and therefore the exchange rates and inflation rates need to be watched to see the effect on the film's budget because the amount of money being handled by a production can result in a marked difference on the returns that changing the money can earn. For example, in high-inflation economies the unit's money should not be changed until the last possible moment, and on a day-to-day basis if necessary. The essential point is that money should be changed at the most advantageous moment for the production and the production's accountant should be able to advise on this matter. An obvious example of the way exchange rates can be used can be seen from the use of Mexico as a location for a recent 'Bond' movie. It may seem extravagant for a major production to take a whole crew to a location like this, but if the script calls for it and the exchange rate allows for sets to be built at a much reduced cost then the financial balance may make it more economic than flying the unit back and forth. Further, it is not only Third World economies that can provide economic benefits. In recent years Toronto and many other parts of Canada have been inundated with US productions (*Mrs Soffel*, *The Fly*) because the locations look American and, at the time these films were made, the exchange rate gave a ratio of five Canadian dollars to four American ones, and any exchange rate becomes meaningful when the budgets are measured in millions.

In a country with a problem economy there will almost certainly be a black market exchange rate but the use of this service should generally be rejected. Dealings with it can result in more trouble than it is worth, not to mention its unreliability. Besides which the production's business is to make films — not to speculate on the local money market and flout the local law.

EQUIPMENT HIRE

When considering the hire of equipment there are a number of factors to be evaluated and this will have an effect on where the equipment is hired and what is hired.

The people who know best what is wanted are the technicians who will be operating the hardware and therefore they should be consulted at an early stage of the production. An experienced crew will already have contacts with those companies which provide equipment and facilities and a lot of time can be saved by using this expertise. This should not mean that every item asked for should be granted; after all the production manager has to consider the whole film.

The other expertise that a production manager should call on is the hire company itself. Provided they are given the opportunity, good companies can give a production a great deal of support but they need the time to do this, so the earlier a contact is made with a hire company the better even if this first contact is only the briefest of outlines about the production.

Generally speaking, hire companies like to be able to fulfil four criteria and these are: preparation, availability or choice, service and back-up.

Equipment can be supplied at short notice but no hire company will be really happy to do this because its reputation relies on the equipment arriving in a fit state and working properly once on the location. Without a reasonable time to prepare the equipment the hire company cannot guarantee that the cameras and recorders will work to the level they are supposed to. In order to be sure of good results the equipment has to be properly prepared and this means giving notice of the requirement.

Notice is also needed if the production is going to be sure that everything that is wanted will be available. This requirement extends not only to the technicians' own preferences for particular equipment but also to the need for any specialist items which may need to be made for the production. This kind of demand is unlikely to be made on a documentary shoot but the director or lighting camera person on a feature may see the film in such a style that the only way to obtain it is by the creation of specialist equipment. The larger hire companies will certainly provide this service but they will need time to do so. Specific items of equipment cannot be engineered at a moment's notice.

As well as specialist services there is the basic question of service in general. A production manager needs to be sure that the film's schedule and other requirements will not be put out by the failure of the hire company to provide a good service, and 'good service' is more than simply providing the right equipment. Besides ensuring that the hire company does what is asked of it promptly, a production manager wants to be reassured that the hirer knows about carnets, import and export legislation, freight services and the many other facilities that may be needed by an overseas shoot, as well as being certain that maintenance facilities can be supplied during a shoot or, in the event of a breakdown, replacement equipment can be delivered quickly. All these are aspects of the service needed by a production and this service is of no value unless it can be backed up.

Back-up means that wherever the shoot is going, at home or abroad, the production company knows that the hire company will give continued support to the film. This support can extend from simply providing a spare piece of equipment, like an extra camera body, to a maintenance engineer to go with the shoot. During the production of *Air America*, which was shot on a foreign location, the unit hired no less than fifteen cameras to cover the various work to be done on the film and overall they had well over 300 boxes of equipment with them on the shoot.

This level of production demand cannot be serviced or supported at short notice and it is unreasonable and unprofessional for a production manager to expect it.

It may be wondered why the production above should want this number of cameras. The answer is that no film wants so many cameras but the production needed equipment for five shooting units, and two back-up cameras were provided for each unit in case of technical problems; the two back-up cameras were required as a form of insurance. Productions which go to locations where a long time may be required to get equipment into and out of the country do not want to have shooting held up because a camera, or any other piece of equipment, goes down and the production has to wait for days or weeks before a replacement is allowed into the country.

It should be remembered that technicians invariably like to have everything 'just in case' but this should not be granted automatically. Equally so, reasonable requests, with supporting arguments showing why a particular item of equipment is needed, should not be refused on the basis of the simplistic argument 'we can't afford it'. Technicians will not work happily if they think they are not worth the equipment they want. Therefore it is necessary to show why the item cannot be afforded rather than reject it out of hand.

The decision on what to hire and who to hire it from should be based on value for money and a clear idea of what is wanted in the final film, but, by now, it should be realized that value for money can extend beyond the immediate rate for the equipment on hire. A cheap hire rate may not save money in the long run.

Good hire companies, provided they are given time to prepare, can supply, service and support any production, however complex.

CHAPTER 14

FURTHER PREPARATION FOR THE SHOOT

As the date for commencement of filming draws closer, so items which seemed less important a few days or weeks before begin to press for attention. Insurances, crew contracts, health and safety and all the other pieces of information which need to be given to the unit and cast have to be finalized.

INSURANCES

Recently a well-respected producer was approached by a colleague and asked what insurances might be needed by a production. After some discussion the producer was prompted to ask his colleague when the production was scheduled to begin shooting. The colleague replied that they were already into their third week! At the bare minimum this is already 4 weeks too late and the colleague was lucky to get away without loss.

Insurances are far too important to be left undone and under item O in Figure 10.1, the feature budget form, there is a key list of the insurances a production is likely to need.

Because of the nature of the business there cannot be a definitive list of insurances required by all productions, for what is necessary on a feature may not be needed on a documentary and what is required by a documentary which is shooting on an overseas location will not be wanted by a feature film being shot in a studio in Britain, so the best people to give advice regarding insurances are the specialist brokers who deal with insurances; their names can be found in all the industry directories.

However, a basic understanding of the main insurances is useful, if only to help decide what might be required by the production.

FILM PRODUCERS' INDEMNITY

This is the generic term used today for the insurances summarized in the first six items on the list in the feature budget form and these insurances are as follows.

Pre-production indemnity and cast insurance

This policy is used more extensively on drama productions as it indemnifies the production company against the additional costs that would be incurred if the production is held up or abandoned because of an accident, or sickness, or death of a specified person during the period of principal photography and sometimes for a period before the beginning of the shoot.

On a documentary the director would usually expect to be insured and on a feature the cover would be extended to principal artistes and any one else whose incapacity might cause the production major problems. For example, it may be important to insure an actor in a character role if the part is spread from the beginning to the end of the shoot rather than a major star who is appearing for a single day's work. One of the usual requirements for this insurance is a medical examination of the insured person. In most contemporary policies an abandonment extension is automatically provided.

Film producers' indemnity

Over the years this insurance has become more sophisticated as film insurance has become more specialized. Initially it only covered the producer against loss if the production ran into specified problems beyond the producers' control. These days it usually includes the pre-production and cast insurance as well as extra expense insurance as part of the standard package.

Consequential loss

These days this policy is known as extra expense and is intended to cover the increased production costs resulting from some vital prop, set or place of equipment being damaged, which in turn means loss of production time and consequently extra costs, i.e. extra expense. In a sense it is a similar policy to cast insurance. The period of the policy should run from the moment the loss of any insured item would cause a cost to the film, so in reality it usually begins when the set construction is first commenced and continues until the end of filming. Any item which, if lost of damaged, may have an adverse effect on the cost of the film should be included and this might mean extending the policy to cover the breakdown of equipment like generators.

Abandonment risk extension

Currently this cover is automatically included in the pre-production indemnity policy.

Errors and omissions

The range of material covered by films, particularly documentaries, means that the company needs to be sure that any third-party claims arising from possible slander, libel, defamation, infringement of copyright, plagiarism, invasion of privacy, incorrect use of formats, titles and ideas are addressed.

Generally this policy would be put in place by the first day of photography and should continue for the active life of the production. This can mean throughout its life in distribution, exhibition and exploitation, depending on contractual requirements. Certainly legal advice is needed during the preparation of a proposal form for this cover and the broker's advice should also be heeded.

Negative insurance (including faulty stock and faulty processing)

This is designed to cover the consequential loss and costs of reshooting any part of a production because of loss or damage to the film or videotape, be it raw stock or processed negative, and to the magnetic tape or sound stock.

Clearly the business of reshooting is very expensive and until the original or negative material is in safe hands and has been copied it needs to be properly covered.

Employer's liability

This insurance is required by law in the United Kingdom and covers the production company in respect of its legal liability for the injury, death, illness or disease of any employees resulting from their employment. This insurance includes any crew or cast engaged on short-term or freelance contracts. This policy has to be taken out as soon as the production company takes on any employees and it should be continued as long as there is anyone on the payroll.

If there are any stunts on the production then the broker's advice should be sought because their work will certainly fall outside any standard employer's liability insurance, and one fact a production manager can be sure of is that stunt personnel will not work without the correct insurance, although they usually carry their own insurance.

Public liability (also known as third-party liability)

This policy indemnifies the production company against third-party claims and generally should run parallel with the employers' liability policy. The insurance covers both property damage and personal injury and the extent of cover may vary depending on the location or facilities being used. The production manager should be aware of the likely costs that a third-party claim may bring. For example, filming in a stately home will have a higher risk than filming in a modern bungalow, and the company should advise the insurance brokers accordingly.

Third-party property damage

This is an insurance designed to cover a production company's legal liability for the damage or loss to a third-party's property which is in their care, custody and control. The most likely situation is accidental damage to a location although it can also cover the cost of hired items if they are damaged and the hire fee has to continue while they are repaired. It should be noted that this policy may cover some of the same ground as the public liability policy and advice should be taken to ensure that there is no duplication.

Equipment—all risks

The equipment on a film is expensive and this policy is designed to cover it, unless the hiring company is already doing so, but if the production is going to exotic locations the insurer, either through the brokers or directly, needs to be told because of possible exclusion clauses. Indeed, as with all insurances, the policy may prove to be invalid if the underwriter has not been given information relevant to the likely risks involved. The cover should be held as long as hired items are being used.

Sets, wardrobe and properties

Like the above insurance for equipment this is an all-risks policy which covers the above items used by the production against damage or theft. It will cover the building of sets and the hire or making of props and costumes. The cover should begin as soon as work starts on any of these items and should continue as long as constructed or hired items are being used.

Action vehicles—motor insurance

A fairly straightforward policy but certainly needed if action vehicles are to be used as the risks are bound to be greater. Motor insurance should also be extended to cover camera cars and any other vehicles involved in the production if they are not properly covered. Therefore it is sensible to check with anyone involved in servicing the production, catering companies for example, to be sure that they have the correct cover.

Cash in transit/money insurance

Depending on the size of the production there may be substantial amounts of cash being handled by the production company and this policy usually covers against loss while the money is in the hands of particular employees. It is advisable for this cover to run from the moment cash is needed on the production until it is completed.

Fidelity guarantee

As the title of this policy states it is cover for a guarantee of faithful performance of duty and most usually is asked for by backers regarding specific persons on the production. It is intended to cover against fraud and embezzlement.

Union insurance

The production company is obliged to take out this insurance in accordance with the producers (PACT) and union agreement. The policy covers crews and cast who are travelling abroad against such risks as sickness, personal accident, temporary life insurance, medical expenses and baggage, and the benefits to be provided are set out in the appropriate agreements.

If a production is not going abroad the union would still expect the company to provide cover for personal accident, especially if any of the performers or technicians are going to be involved in dangerous or hazardous work such as filming from helicopters or in storms. This should certainly include filming stunts.

Foreign insurance

If a production is going overseas to a foreign location it is wise to discuss with the brokers what kind of risks may be incurred by the production company and decide if insurance is needed.

Other insurances

The above list essentially covers the requirements of the average film production. However, there is no such thing as an average production and as such insurances may be needed for aeroplanes (aviation), boats or ships (marine), animals (livestock), weather, kidnap and ransom (in some parts of the world) and political risks (contract frustration) in places where the film may be deemed to be sensitive by the resident power.

In all insurance matters the brokers should be consulted and heeded, for they are in the business to help get the right answers for the individual productions, but if there is any particular recommendation to be made to producers and production managers it simply is this: do *not* try and save money by not taking out insurance — it should not even be thought of. It is a false economy and, in any case, if a production has been properly budgeted the money should be there for insurance.

CREW HIRE—LETTER OF ENGAGEMENT

Sam Goldwyn reportedly said that 'A verbal contract isn't worth the paper it is written on' and consequently film crews want to see their contract before they begin. This can most easily be accomplished by sending a letter of engagement to the person concerned. The letter should specify under which rate card the production is being made and consequently this will be the basis of the contract. There is a model letter of engagement included in the agreements and it looks like the following.

Address of Technician,
Date of letter.

Dear ...

We have pleasure in confirming the terms and conditions of your employment with the company in the grade of ... [grade of post being offered] and based at ... [the address from where the production company is operating].

1. This engagement is subject to the terms and conditions of the current PACT/BECTU Freelance Production Agreement, or as may be amended by the parties to that agreement, a copy of which is available for your inspection at ... [usually the production office address].
2. Your engagement commences on ... [date] and will be subject to a 2 week period of notice prior to termination.
3. Your weekly salary for the Basic Weekly Hours (Basic Daily Hours) will be £ .... . Any work beyond these hours shall be paid at the appropriate overtime rate. Any hours of overtime (beyond the agreed hours per day) will be paid for at the appropriate rate. If on resident location you will be paid a minimum of 4 hours at single time for the rest day as stand-by payment.
4. Your holiday pay entitlements/credits and your entitlements to paid benefit during the period absence due to sickness or injury are as laid down in the PACT/BECTU Freelance Production Agreement. For statutory sick pay scheme purposes qualifying days will be ... [date] to ... [date].
5. The period of notice required to be given or received to terminate your engagement will be as specified in the PACT/BECTU Freelance Production Agreement provided that such notice is not less favourable than current legislation.
6. You confirm that you are and will remain during the period of engagement a British subject ordinarily domiciled in the United

Kingdom, and that you are a member of the appropriate Trade Union in good standing.

7. You will not pledge the credit of the Company or order goods or incur any liabilities on the Company without specific authority.

8. During the period of this engagement we shall be entitled to your services and all the products thereof and all the rights therein shall be and remain our exclusive property. There is no guarantee that the production or any part thereof will necessarily proceed to completion or that you are engaged for the duration of the production period.

9. If you have any grievance relating to your employment you should raise the matter, either orally or in writing with ... [usually the production manager].

10. If you are in agreement with the terms and conditions stated above will you kindly sign the enclosed copy of this letter where indicated and return it to us with your details of employment form duly completed.

FOR AND ON BEHALF OF ....

[including the employing company's name]

SIGNED ....
[include name and position]

11. I hereby agree to the terms and conditions of my agreement as stated above and confirm that I am and will remain a British subject for the duration of my engagement.

SIGNED ....

DATE ....

This model letter, which is a variation on the one in the union agreements, is only the basis for an engagement and can be adapted to meet the requirements of a particular production, provided both parties agree to the alterations.

Just as crews should be concerned about starting a production without a letter of engagement, so production managers should be worried if they have not had a signed one returned. The letter defines the working conditions and signing it confirms the trust of both parties. No signature probably means no trust and this means no good even before the production has started.

HEALTH AND SAFETY

The production agreements formally cover matters of health and safety but, from the point of view of the project, it is important for the crew to be fit for work regardless of where the location is and, having solved the problem of getting a crew to a location, it is clearly important to keep the crew members fit once they are there. This is not a real problem for locations local to the production office but as the locations spread further from the production base and become more 'exotic' then there is an increased likelihood of difficulties arising, especially if the location is outside the temperate zones.

Generally speaking the nearer the Equator the location is the more likely the requirement for vaccinations or injections of one sort or another. Malaria, yellow fever and other illnesses are still rife in many parts of the world and under the agreements the production is obliged to protect the crews going to these places. So at the very least medical advice must be taken even if a nurse or doctor is not included on the crew. In instances where the production is shooting stunts or other dangerous work it may be required and certainly is advisable to have medical assistance standing by.

Because the dangers of tropical climates are obvious it does not mean that the polar regions are trouble free. Temperatures in locations inside the Arctic and Antarctic Circles can be so low that a few minutes outside without proper protection can result in death. Again expert advice should be taken.

It is impossible to consider all the different problems that may face a production going on an overseas location; suffice it to say that the production manager's chief concern is to ensure the smooth running of the filming and this means, amongst other things, that no one on the unit comes to harm.

WEATHER AND GEOGRAPHY

Part of the process of evaluating a production, particularly for an overseas shoot, involves an understanding of the location in terms of its weather and geography. This is probably best explained in the following three simple examples. Firstly a location shoot in India: the questions that have to be asked are where and when, because geography should have provided information about the monsoon season and, unless the monsoon is an integral part of the production, it will severely interfere with the filming. Secondly a location shoot in Northern Canada: the question to consider here is transport and particularly at a time of emergency, for this is a region, like the Australian outback, the Amazon jungle, the Himalayas and other similar areas in the world, where what would be an uncomplicated accident in a populated area can present a number of difficulties when occurring in a remote location. Thirdly a tropical location: in general both the weather and geography need to be looked at for there are places in the tropics which, because of their height, are far from warm and other places which, because of their position, have a very regular weather pattern, such as a rainstorm every day during the wet season. The point that the production manager should keep in mind is that time spent considering the problems likely to arise from working in a particular place is time well spent if, because of this preparation, action can be taken to counteract possible problems rather than having to waste time in dealing with the 'unexpected' when it occurs.

Planning for the unexpected is one of the jobs of the production manager and one of the ways of dealing with the cost implications is by having proper insurances.

UNION CLEARANCES

In cases where a production is going overseas the union should be advised and clearances received, as the employing company is a member of PACT or a signatory to the agreements. This is a requirement under rule 19 of the union's rules. On a feature film this matter will be dealt with at the pre-production meeting but on documentary productions the form outlined in Appendix C of the Freelance Production Agreement should be used and forwarded to the union office.

This may appear to be union bureaucracy but the union can only help a production that has troubles overseas, if it is aware of the unit's departure and has been properly consulted at the pre-production meeting.

THE PRE-PRODUCTION MEETING

This is a meeting between the employers' association and the unions to confirm that the terms of the agreements between both sides are being complied with and that there are no outstanding problems which may jeopardize the start or continuance of a production. The unions represented are BECTU, EEPTU, British Equity and possibly the MU and FAA; for the employers the Producers' Alliance for Cinema and Television (PACT) and IPPA or ITVA are usually represented, depending on the production.

The chief matters discussed at the pre-production meeting will usually cover the following points: the schedule and working hours, particularly the likely overtime as the unions do not like to see their members being exploited and do not want them to be working excessively long hours; the crew and cast lists, to ensure that the people employed are bona fide members; money in escrow or guarantees, to confirm that the financial position of the production is sufficiently stable so that the employees will be paid and that the producer will not have a lot of work done only to disappear without paying any bills; and locations, as the union will want to know where they are, how safe they are and, if there are any dangers, what precautions have been taken to protect the crew and cast.

Individual productions may well have other points which the unions will want clarifying: explosive special effects, for example, but generally the Producer and Production Manager should welcome any advice or guidance that is given because in the end the unions, like good producers, want the production to run smoothly and without accidents, incompetence or financial trouble.

Following the agreement between the unions and employers that all is in order, the production is in a position to go ahead.

CHAPTER 15

THE SHOOT

This is the time when it is discovered if all the preparation has paid off or not.

The only way a production manager knows if the preparation has succeeded is if the shoot goes smoothly, although it should be noted that this does not necessarily mean that the shoot goes precisely to plan. It should be more a case of the plans being sufficiently flexible that they can accommodate any last-minute changes without unduly affecting the overall scheme of the production. This is one area where properly scheduled pick-up times can pay full dividends.

In order for the scheme not to be unduly upset the shoot must be kept under control and this means using similar disciplines to those used for keeping a budget under control, firstly by keeping track of the progress of the production.

PROGRESS REPORTS

The best way to keep track of what is happening during filming is to note on the production's progress reports the coming and goings of anyone and everyone involved in the film. The larger the shoot the more important it is for every detail to be noted and recorded because these records form a diary of the production and can be used at a later date should there be any disputes about the way the production proceeded. Indeed, they can become legal documents in the event of a lawsuit.

Nothing should happen on a shoot without the appropriate sanction being given and noted. An actor on a foreign location with a few free days should not be allowed away from the shoot without written permission and a clear understanding of the conditions of release being agreed. There was a recent incident where this procedure was not followed, with the result that the performer had a 'holiday' in the middle of the shoot and got paid for it because it had never been noted that the actor was away from the location. A visit by one or more of the financiers should be noted in the progress reports, for instance 'Mr X of the completion bond company visited the production today'. Possibly most important of all, any accident which happens to crew or visitors must be noted with the result and what treatment was used. This information will certainly be wanted if there are any insurance claims resulting from the accident.

Therefore the best discipline for progress reports is to start each day with the opening details of the day's work, including all who are present, and to keep notes from that moment to the end of the day.

In Figure 15.1, all the basic information about the scenes completed, footage exposed, artistes' times, additional crew and cast and screen time shot are noted. The notes on the report detail any exceptional activity and indicate why the production might be behind schedule, although the daily average indicates that the schedule will be caught up, as long as the average is maintained.

THE HIERARCHY

Although at first sight film crews seem to be very casual there usually is a well-defined hierarchy on a unit and, as with any job, it is necessary to understand and work within these constraints. The heads of individual departments can instruct their own crews to do whatever they feel is needed but if they require some action from another department then formally it should be requested from the head of that department.

It is a fallacy to think that time will be saved by doing it yourself: a piece of equipment moved from one corner of a set to another without the knowledge of the 'owner' may waste more time in an unnecessary search than was supposedly saved by doing it yourself. In common with every industry the hierarchy has been developed over the years. It has evolved so that those who need to know what is happening do so and consequently can save time by effectively instructing their crews. The worst thing members of a unit can do is to involve themselves in an area which is not their responsibility. This is a total waste of time besides being very annoying and unprofessional. The classic example of how not to behave was demonstrated by a recently graduated film student who, being used to working in every department on student productions, started to suggest to the director of a feature how a shot might be set up, although the graduate was only working as a runner. The graduate was put right very quickly, and learnt a lesson he should have known before he left his film course. Help, if asked, but be cautious about offering advice.

THE CALL SHEET

The chief way of keeping everyone informed of what is happening from day to day is the call sheet. This document must be issued at the latest before the end of the previous day to everyone who is needed on the set on the day in question. Figure 15.2 shows an example.

FUTURA PRODUCTIONS Ltd.

DAILY PROGRESS REPORT NO: 26.

PRODUCTION: "Times Past" **DATE:** Monday 1st. April 2001.
DIRECTOR: Luke Skywalker.

WORKING AT: Windsor Castle.

UNIT CALL: 08:00
FIRST SET-UP: 09:40
LUNCH FROM: 12:50
      TO: 13:50
UNIT DISMISSED 17:55

SCENE NUMBERS SHOT TODAY:
1, 2, 147, 148, 149.

SLATE NUMBERS: 234 to 245.

FILM STOCK RECORD

LOADED	NG	PRINT	EXPOSED	WASTE	SHORT ENDS		SOUND ROLLS
34,800	9,210	22,950	32,160	2,140	500	Previously	50
2,400	860	980	1,840	110	450	Today	2
37,200	10,070	23,930	34,000	2,250	950	Total	52

ARTISTES	DAYS	CALLED	DISMISSED	ADDITIONAL CAST/CREW ETC.	RATE
Harold Godwin	21	07.30	17.55	35 Soldiers	@ Basic
Edith Swaneck	19	07.00	17.55	3 Stand-ins	@ Basic.
Adam Brand	3	07.30	16.00		
+William B'Stard	6	07.30	16.00	2nd. Camera Crew :-	
				Operator - Judge Davis.	
Ivan Odeye	9	10.00	17.55	Focus - Laura Hand.	
Ilse Gunnor	2	06.30	16.00	Loader - George Campbell.	
				Grip - Joe Hunk.	
+ Part Completed.				Prosthetic Make-up Artist:-	
				Maureen Fairweather.	

NOTES: Catering Numbers: 98.
Additional Panaflex Camera on hire.

Joe Hunk dropped a crane weight on his left foot; treated at St.George's Hospital Casualty.

35 minutes shooting time lost P.M. due to Generator failure.

SCHEDULE STATUS

Start Date:	25:2:01
Scheduled Days:	55
Days Shot:	26
Days Remaining:	29
Days Over:	1½
~~Days Under~~	

SCREEN TIME

Previously	55'	30"
Today	2'	40"
Total to Date	58'	10"
Remaining	61'	50"
Total Script	120'	00"
Daily Average:	2'	14"

Ellen Merlin

Ellen Merlin.
PRODUCTION SUPERVISOR

Figure 15.1

   The points to notice on a call sheet should generally be self-evident but it is worth highlighting some practices. It is important to realize that this document goes out under the name of the first assistant director: as they are running the floor it is their responsibility.

```
                                  CALL SHEET                    No.  5

Production: WIZARD
FAIRFAX FILMS Ltd., 40 Yonge Park, London N4 3NT.
Phone: 081 234 5678
Director: Name                                Date: Wed. 25th...
Unit call: 07.30 On location: 08.00
Location:Archaeological site
            Devon Road
            Nr Tintagel
            (see movement order 5)
Sets: None                           Scene Nos: 2,6,108.
On-site production office: Caravan 3, Devon Road.
Phone no: 0987-654321
```

ACTOR	CHARACTER	P/UP	M/UP	ON SET
Name	Richard Fairfax	08.00	08.30	09.30
Name	Melanie Fairfax	08.00	08.30	09.00
Name	Jenny	09.00	09.30	10.30
Name	David	09.00	09.30	10.30
Name	Georgia	12.30	13.00	14.00
Others/extras	Two (Archaeologists)	09.00	09.30	10.30
Stand-ins	Two	08.00	–	08.30

```
Art Dept: As per script and schedule.
Props: As per script and schedule to include: Lead box, crystal
globe.
SP.FX: None.
Make-up: As per script and schedule.
Action vehicles: Richard Fairfax's car.
Catering: Breakfast  - 08.15 to 09.00 for 50
          Coffee     - 10.15 for 55
          Lunch      - 1 hour between 12.30 and 14.00 for 60
          Tea        - 15.30 for 60
Unit car: to pick up A.A. and B.B. from hotel at 08.00.
Transport: Both production buses to leave hotel at 07.30
Notes: Time sheets for this week to be in the production office
       by Tuesday the 31st at the latest.
Name                                    1st Assistant Director
```

Figure 15.2

There is a need to title all documents so that the crews know to which production and what subject the paper applies; this is done on the first five lines of the call sheet. The next eight lines give the basic information for the whole unit and this is followed by specific information for particular people. This usually covers the cast, especially as they may only be on the location for 1 day and consequently do not have the opportunity to discover what is going on from other people on the shoot.

It should be noted that the artiste playing the character Georgia is only called for the afternoon. There is no benefit in having everyone on the set or location who is not going to be working. Artistes spend long enough standing around waiting to be called without the extra tedium of being called sooner than they are needed and, like anyone who feels their time is being wasted, their performance is not improved by being called early and then apparently forgotten. This simply is another case of the need for good 'people' management by the production manager and the first assistant director so that performers are kept in a good mood for work.

This management should extend to advising the cast of the shooting progress throughout the day so that they are kept in touch with the filming and feel part of the crew.

On a feature this exercise in human relations would be undertaken by the second or third assistant director, who is part of the production team. On a documentary, if the director does not do it then the production manager must. Indeed on a documentary shoot this aspect of keeping people informed is even more important because, unlike professional performers who may be used to being, in the words of Alfred Hitchcock, 'treated like cattle', the ordinary public involved in a documentary will eventually resent being ignored, especially if they are being paid nothing, and this resentment will result in a lack of cooperation which in turn may well mean more expense. Therefore deciding the call times on the call sheet should be given careful thought and not dismissed by using the lazy expedient of calling everyone early.

The information following the specific call times should cover any other details which the unit needs to know. This information will be collated from the schedule and usually covers the departments which provide services additional to the basic technical unit, that is the camera crew would expect to use the same camera each day but the props department would expect to be asked for different props on different days, and these requirements should be recorded on the call sheet. For example, in 'Cops and Robbers' programmes there will be a need for guns and this means that an SFX armourer has to be on the set. Specialists, whatever their expertise, have to be given time to prepare if they are going to exercise their skills efficiently.

It would be in the 'notes' section of a call sheet that the publicity department might put information about expected visitors.

One of the incidental benefits of the call sheet is that it helps to give those individuals, like artistes or specialists who are not with the unit on a day-to-day basis, a feeling of being included in and belonging to the production. This sense of teamwork is very important to a project.

MOVEMENT ORDER

The other document which is expected when a unit goes on location is a movement order. This gives the information and instructions about how crew and cast are to get to a location or set and what transport is being provided by the production.

This document usually only applies to feature productions or films of a similar size. A documentary would generally expect to have the unit's transport instructions incorporated into their schedule. A movement order for a feature film may look like Figure 15.3. As before, the document begins with the titling to identify the matter being covered.

In addition to the directions given for finding the location there is also information about what can be done on the location. In the document in Figure 15.3, part of the location is in essence out of bounds, and a professional crew usually understands the need to treat the location with respect. A good location manager will try and ensure that no problems

```
                      MOVEMENT  ORDER                      No.  5

Production:  WIZARD
FAIRFAX  FILMS  Ltd.,  40  Yonge  Park,  London  N4  3NT.
Phone:  081  234  5678
Director:  Name                                       Date:
Location  description/comments:
From  hotel—Take  the  A00  to  ...  [directions  to  location]
                The  distance  is  20  miles  and  takes  approximately  30
                minutes.
                Please  do  not  interfere  with  the  diggings  to  the  NE
                corner  of  the  location.
Car  1—Production  car  1                     Leaves  hotel  @  07.30
(G117  THX)  Driver:  Name
Passenger  1:  Name                      Passenger  2:  Name
Passenger  3:  Name                      Passenger  4:  Name
Car  2  —  Production  car  2                  Leaves  hotel  @  08.00
(G118  THX)  Driver:  Name
Passenger  1:  Name                      Passenger  2:  Name
Passenger  3:  Name                      Passenger  4:  Name
Minibus  1  —  F246  RFG  —  Camera/sound  crew,  leaves  hotel  @  07.30
Minibus  2  —  F248  RFG  —  Make-up/art  dept,  leaves  hotel  @  07.30
Cast  to  be  collected  for  the  afternoon:
Car  1  —  Production  car  1                  Leaves  hotel  @  12.30
(G117  THX)  Driver:  Name
Passenger  1:  Name                      Passenger  2:  Name
Catering  and  toilet  facilities  will  be  provided  on  site
Artistes  rest  room  will  be  available  at  the  location  contact's
house
Contacts:
Location  contact,                       Hospital  with  casualty,
Address  &  phone  no.                   Address  &  phone  no.
Police  contact,                         Generator  suppliers,
Address  &  phone  no.                   Address  &  phone  no.
```

Figure 15.3

arise between the location's owner and the unit, particularly as a location may be used for a period of time during the filming. Also the location manager may want to use the same location in future and for this reason alone the area should be respected, especially if the crew members want to promote their chances of further work.

THE RELEASE FORM

During the filming of any production permission has to be obtained by the film company for the use of the images recorded by it.

When a location is used the contract covering the use of the site will include permission to use the recorded footage. The contract with an artiste will also include this permission. However, there are times when no prior contract has been signed or permission given. Therefore in order to be sure that there is no comeback on the production the production office should get a release form signed. The format for this document, which should be printed on the company's note paper, is basically as shown in Figure 15.4.

This release form is most commonly used by documentary productions which involve 'vox pops' or, in other words, people speaking in the street and giving their opinion of the subject in the programme. Sometimes feature films may involve uncontracted performers, Richard Lester's *The Knack* is an example, and whenever a performance is given

```
                        RELEASE FORM

   I  [Name].......................
   of  [Address]....................
   agree to perform in the film provisionally titled [Working title
   of the production] being made by [Name of production company].
   I agree that the film may be shown, exhibited or exploited in any
   media or territory as required by the production company.
   I understand that no fee/a fee of £ ... [whichever is applicable]
   is payable for this performance and that I have no further claim
   on the production company or any other person associated with this
   production.

   Signed  ........

   Date  ..........

   Witness  ........
```

Figure 15.4

permission to use it must be obtained. The purpose of the form is to get a written and agreed clearance by the performer that his or her comments may be used in the film without that person later suing the production company for 'mis-using' his or her volunteered comments.

Television companies certainly require evidence that all the material in a production is free of encumbrances and therefore would want to know that all interviewees who did not have a prior contract would have signed a release form. Indeed any film maker who hopes to have the production shown for commercial gain needs to ensure that anyone involved in the production has no further claims on the film.

This is a point often overlooked by film students who are subsequently disappointed when their work is not shown because of the possible additional cost of paying artistes in their productions and because those people have not signed release forms. Essentially it is an instant contract in which, either for no payment or for a limited payment, the person signing it gives up all rights to a commercial interest in the production.

PUBLICITY

The publicity team will present one of the ongoing areas for control on a shoot. Its job is to get the production as well known as possible and this means bringing the press, radio and television journalists, the critics, backers, sponsors and any other people who may help the promotion of the production on to the set. However, there are times when the last thing the director or crew needs is a stranger or, worse, a group of them rubber necking their way round. The result is that the set may occasionally be closed to outsiders. Therefore it is essential that the production office is informed about potential visitors before they decide to visit. It is a matter of courtesy to inform the director in advance of all visitors, even if not actually asking their permission. Also, the artists should be informed of any visiting journalists who may wish to interview them.

As ever, this comes back to giving out information. If the publicity department knows when the set is going to be closed then they will not, or should not, arrive with an important critic in tow.

CHAPTER 16

POST-PRODUCTION

With the completion of the shoot the time of greatest pressure on a production is probably over. However, this is not the time to relax because, as mentioned earlier, there may still be pressure on the editorial team to meet the delivery date.

The people involved in pre-production, the shooting crew and some of the assistants in the production office hopefully will move on to another film, but the production manager still has to see the film through the post-production phase. In the first instance, this means taking it through the editing period.

EDITING

Once the shoot has finished the filmed material must be organized into script order; this is the beginning of the editing process.

However, this process involves a number of elements each of which has to be managed and controlled. The production manager will have planned a schedule for the editing period during the pre-production phase of the project. This schedule will now be re-evaluated in the light of the information gained during the shoot and in conjunction with the film's editor.

The editorial process is the direct responsibility of the editor who will want to define the needs of the editorial team in order that the process can be completed efficiently.

It should be realized that the editing process is more involved than simply putting the printed footage into its final order. Firstly, editing is an artistic process requiring knowledge, judgement and talent. Secondly the editor has to be aware of the many pieces that go towards creating the final film. These will include the sound, music, special optical effects and any other work that needs to be done before the film or programme can be completed. For example, sound transfers will be required, and the chosen transfer facility will need to know all the relevant production information to complete the job: film running speed 24 or 25 and so on. This is equally true for video edits, where information about time coding is essential before work can begin.

It is at this stage that one of the major differences between film and video production emerges. The editing process for video takes place in two stages: the 'off line' edit, followed by the 'on line' edit. The production manager has to be aware of the relative costs of these stages. The 'on line' edit can cost as much in an hour as a day's 'off line' editing, and the daily hire of an 'off line' edit suite can cost as much as the weekly hire for a film cutting room. However, these extra costs for editing video are usually more than balanced by the additional cost of purchasing and processing film. Nevertheless the control of video editing costs has to be watched carefully, and it is because of the expense of 'on line' editing that time is spent doing the initial editing in an 'off line' suite. Like most production work the time spent in preparing for the 'on line' edit is time well spent, because an hour wasted in the 'on line' suite can be a very expensive hour indeed. Any method of saving time should be welcomed.

One of the aids that an editor and a director will need is a copy of the script as shot. In documentary terms this is a transcription of all the interviews, commentary and other spoken parts.

TRANSCRIPTION

During the shooting of a drama film any script lines that are altered will be noted by the continuity person. The alterations may be minimal but need to be noted if a correct post-production script is to be prepared and sometimes this script is required by the contract. These notes will also help the editor find the right footage for the scene he or she is working on. For a documentary the transcription is vital for seeing what the interviewees say and consequently for editing it into a more compact or coherent narrative. The time saved by initially editing the transcription usually outweighs the expense of getting the tapes transcribed, and has the advantage that the material is readily available for the post-production script. The post-production script is usually prepared from the answer print but, as ever, any work done earlier in the production can help to save time at a later stage.

SOUND

The tradition in most film-making countries is to record the sound at the same time as shooting the film but there are some places, Italy being the best example, where the dialogue is re-recorded in a studio and this and all the other sounds are put on after the shooting has been completed with the sound recorded during the shoot being used as a guide track.

There are other instances where voices are post-synchronized and these include songs in musical films or the dubbing of different languages on to the track so that the film can be distributed more widely. These are occasions where a post-production script will be needed.

Even if the dialogue is not re-recorded there is the matter of mixing all the other sound effects. All this work can only be done properly in sound studios equipped for the job, generally known as re-recording theatres or rooms. Obviously these have to be booked in advance and, as with every other part of the schedule, this means careful pre-planning has to take place so that time is not wasted, particularly as good mixing theatres can be expensive to hire. Also, if a particular mixing engineer is required, the final timing of the mix can be crucial.

One of the parts of the mixing process is the incorporation of music into the film. Music is an important ingredient of any production yet it is often overlooked, especially on lower-budget productions. The importance of music cannot be overstressed. Whether the music is from the classics, like the Mozart score in *Elvira Madigan,* or specially composed for a film, name your favourite theme from a particular film and then recall that someone chose or composed the piece. The reasons why music is overlooked are many and various but the creative film maker will want the right music to go with the images and this requires time for thought and preparation before it can be recorded.

MUSIC RECORDING

Music recording is the responsibility of the music director in conjunction with the production manager.

Assuming the production is having music specially recorded for the film, then there will be one or more recording sessions. The music director, like the heads of the other departments, will be recommending who should be employed and where the recording should be done although it is the production office which will arrange the details and issue the contracts. Therefore the production manager needs to be aware of the particular requirements for musicians and also needs time to arrange for these requirements to be met. Like actors and actresses, top-class musicians are not usually available at a moment's notice.

One ploy that has been used in an effort to save money is to record in those countries where a once and for all payment overcomes the problems of royalties and residuals. Although attractive initially, it is not without potential dangers and certainly requires more time and planning to bring to fruition.

If music is bought 'off the shelf' then three things have to be done. First of all someone, usually the director, has to listen to the music and make the necessary choices. Then the production office has to sort out the clearances required so that the music can be used by the production. This means getting in touch with the Mechanical Copyright Protection Society (MCPS) for copying permission and the Performing Rights

Society (PRS) for copyright permission. Finally a time has to be arranged for the music to be transferred to magnetic film or videotape so that the sound editor can incorporate it into the editing process.

SPECIAL EFFECTS

The special effects required for a production can range from the relatively simple to the highly complex and in the latter case may present a situation where, like in the film *Star Wars*, the preparation and production of these effects may take longer to achieve than the original shooting.

In modern films there are so many different ways of achieving on the screen what the director wants that it is unlikely that any one individual will have all the answers. Therefore, as with all specializations in the industry, the production manager should consult with the experts as early as possible about what will be needed so that proper planning can take place.

Different kinds of special effect need their own time frame to be realized. Some effects have to be ready before shooting commences. This is particularly true of productions which have complex forms of make-up, such as *Planet of the Apes* or *The Elephant Man*, or films which use animatronics, such as *ET* or *Dark Crystal*. These productions cannot begin until this preparation is completed.

Films which incorporate laboratory effects in their production also have to give the laboratories time to prepare for the work. A fade or dissolve will be part of the laboratory's standard catalogue but the visual special effects or opticals in a film like *Star Wars* require a lot of planning and no laboratory will achieve good results if it is asked to produce work at short notice. It will try but it will not guarantee to do so. One of the special effects required by every production is in the form of the title sequence.

TITLES

The titles on a film, like everything else, need to be planned for in advance.

This is because there are the questions of who, in what order, how long, in what style and other points that have to be considered before the material can be prepared for shooting. There may also be some contractual requirements to be fulfilled. It should be realized that the contracts of some major stars extend to defining how and where their names will arrive in the title sequence and what size of lettering will be used. Similar requirements will be made for technical credits like the Dolby Stereo logo, Panasonic logo and film stock logos. The logos will be supplied by their owners. These details have to be acted on, as with all contractual points.

The design and production of effective titles cannot be completed at short notice and a film cannot be delivered without the titles.

Although every film will have titles there are some needs which will only apply to particular films, and one of these is the use of library material.

LIBRARY MATERIAL

The commonest use of library material is in the production of documentary films, although feature films may also need to use this kind of footage.

The researcher, having found the film needed, will also have to advise the production office of the terms for the purchase of the rights to use the material. The usual terms are based on a payment for a minute, or part thereof, of footage and the rate depends on the extent of use of the material.

Thus a single broadcast in the UK will be cheaper than a single broadcast to the UK and Europe and the rate will rise with every 'territory' that is asked for until the whole world is covered. It will also rise if more than one medium is used, so the rights for broadcast will be cheaper than those for broadcast and videotape. This, in turn, is cheaper than cable, satellite, videotape and broadcast. Therefore the easiest way of dealing with the matter is to buy the rights to all 'territories' and all media so that the film can be shown anywhere in the world in any form ranging from the cinema through television on videotape, broadcast, satellite and cable and any other method yet to be invented. Only if the producer knows that the programme will never be seen on a particular medium or in a specific country might it be worth negotiating a lesser agreement, but generally speaking to negotiate for anything less than all rights will hamper the exploitation possibilities of the programme. Therefore it is not worth it.

With the completion of all the stages above the editing process will be coming to an end and the results have to be married together. This is done at the mix.

THE MIX

Like most of the processes in the production of a film the mixing of sound, dialogue, music and effects track appears to be a simple operation but, without proper preparation, it can easily go astray.

As it is part of the editorial process the mix usually is managed by the editor, but as it is part of the production the production manager must be on hand to ensure that the editor receives the back-up required. On the editor's advice the production office should book the re-recording theatre, ensure that any post-sync dubbing or revoicing cast are available and check the contractual clauses covering artiste revoicing. Confirm that equipment or material for special sound effects is to hand and generally make sure that time will not be wasted in the dubbing theatre because of lack of planning. Footstep or Foley artistes are very time-consuming, but are essential for a full M and E track.

The crew in a re-recording theatre has a lot of expertise to give to a film but, in common with the individuals involved in all the other areas of a production, it can only give its best if it has been informed of what is expected. Part of this information is provided by the dubbing cue chart. The important point to remember here is that the chart should be as clear and comprehensive as possible. As with a shoot, it is far cheaper for the assistant editor to redraw a chart than to have a dubbing crew standing around while the editor, director and others concerned decide what is wanted from the mix.

The other major decision to be made prior to the mix is what result is required. In other words will a 'music and effects' (M & E) track be needed or can all the sound be married together in one recording? The answer to this question will depend on the likely market of the production. If it is a programme which is expected to get overseas sales, then there will be a requirement for enabling a foreign language dub on to the soundtrack. This means that all the music and effects should be mixed together to provide the ideal M & E track and then this in turn will be married to the dialogue tracks. If at a later date a foreign language version is wanted then only the dialogue tracks need to be recorded.

It should be noted that if a special process sound treatment is wanted, for example, Dolby Stereo or Ultra Stereo, then the required contracts and fees for the licence have to be drawn up and payments settled before any mixing can begin.

In addition to the producer, director and editor the other crew member at the mix should be the sound recordist/mixer. This is not always possible with freelance staff but good management, if not courtesy, should mean that the recordist is invited; this is assuming that the recordist is not already contracted to be there, which may be the case for a feature but is unlikely on a tight documentary budget.

On completion of the mix the sound track must be transferred to optical negative. For 16 mm film this is always mono, but the 'winding' of the sound negative ('A' or 'B') should be checked with the laboratory. For 35 mm film there is the choice of mono or stereo sound, but again, it is worth checking to ensure that the stereo optical facilities are available when you want them. The film should now be ready to be returned to the laboratories for the final print to be produced.

THE PRINT

The production of the print is the penultimate stage in the creation of a film and, as far as the production office is concerned, the preparation needed is similar to that used for the dubbing process.

The laboratory used for the final print has to have all the material in its possession. This includes the cut negative, the soundtrack, the titles and any other special effects material which may have been produced outside the laboratory's own walls.

Again the producer, director and editor would expect to be at the viewing of the answer prints. Also the director of photography or lighting camera person should be invited to these viewings. On a feature film the heads of departments would expect to be present at any stage which affected their department but, as noted above, this may not always be possible on productions which have very tight budgets. However, the production manager should invite the departmental heads and let them decide if they can afford to be at the screening.

With the acceptance of a final answer print the laboratory is in a position to deliver show prints and the production has now reached a stage where it can meet one of the key points negotiated during the financing of the project, that is the delivery date.

CHAPTER 17

DELIVERY

The delivery of a film is the end of the production process and is a key date as far as a producer is concerned. It is also a key date for the production manager as it indicates the time by which all the business of the production should be complete.

With the delivery most of the remaining crew who are still employed, usually the freelance editorial and production staff, will be given their finishing dates and will, hopefully find further work on other productions.

However, the producer and the production office may still have work to do because delivery is more than handing over a copy of the film. There are a number of requirements which have to be met and the tying up of all these possible loose ends is the business of the production manager. It should be realized that, in terms of good business practice, it is easier to sort these matters out as they arise and not leave them to the end of the production. This is because it is far harder to get details from individuals who have been involved in the film after they have left the production. Researchers who have gone away to other work, performers who are in other productions, locations which cannot be returned to easily and all sorts of other information which people have and take away with them are examples in point. The obvious answer is to grab them while they are on the set.

Therefore the production manager has to be aware of any outstanding paperwork if delivery is to be completed properly. This paperwork includes the accounts, clearances and publicity material, these being the usual delivery conditions after the delivery date.

DELIVERY DATE

The delivery date will be specified in the original contract and there will almost certainly be penalties if the date is not met. These penalties will vary but usually have a financial component, although there may be other terms as well. These other terms can affect a film maker in a way which may seem to be worse than any financial terms. For example,

Ridley Scott, a director of some reputation, (The Dualists, Alien, Blade Runner), apparently delivered *Legend* a few days late with the result that the financing studio recut the film. Scott was unable to do anything to stop this action because the studio argued — rightly — that the late delivery, even though it was only a matter of a few days, had broken his contract. Because they were unhappy with the shape of the film the consequent breach of contract allowed them to change it to a form they thought was better, although it was certainly not the director's concept of the film.

The delivery date will be a key clause of the contract but it needs to be understood that this is more than some arbitary decision by the backer. The date for the film to be delivered can be crucial if it is to do well on the cinema circuit. A production aimed at the children's market which is not finished in time for the right release date, usually a holiday period, may end up failing to make an impact on this market.

In the case of television companies the delivery date is equally important. Schedules are planned months in advance and have to be met. Therefore the film has to be delivered on time if the television company is to be sure it is getting the programme it has commissioned.

DELIVERY CONDITIONS

As indicated above, the prime delivery condition is the delivery date but there are also other conditions which have to be met if the film is to be acceptable to the financier. Most of these conditions will be specified in the contract but some will be there by implication.

The best example of this is the standard request that the film be delivered free of all encumbrances. A film delivered under these conditions promises the backer that the film can be shown without anyone making any additional claims on the production. It implies that the necessary clearances have been negotiated and that no one will be claiming additional payments or if there have to be any additional payments these have already been negotiated and are known. This latter case applies to advertising films where performers are given a further payment every time the advert is shown. It is not only the performers who might receive these payments. The composers of advertising jingles also get paid for each instance their music is played. Indeed there is at least one composer who likes to include a whistling tune in his jingles which he usually performs, Result: two payments every time the tune is heard.

In order for the contracting company to deliver the film free of all encumbrances the production manager will have had to obtain the necessary clearances. One of the reasons why television companies have a completion date well in advance of the scheduled broadcast date is so they can be sure that the necessary clearances have been obtained before the production is finally allowed on air.

CLEARANCES

A financing company has no wish to be involved in breach of copyright cases, in the non-payment of fees or invoices for any contracted work or any other legal wrangles. Therefore it will want to be assured that all the various rights have been cleared and that there are no outstanding matters to be settled. This assurance will have to be in the form of documentary evidence. If this evidence is not available then the production company may have to write a letter accepting all responsibility for any claim against the film.

The first of the rights to be considered is the ownership of the original script. In the case of an original idea this should present less of a problem as the producer should hold the initial contract with the writer, but if the film is an adaptation of the work by a living author or a writer whose work is still in copyright then evidence of the ownership of the film rights will be required before the first contracts are even signed. Therefore a film of a book will involve getting the film rights to the book and the rights to use a script based on the book.

The next major area for rights is in the use of music. Again if the music is originally composed and recorded for the film then the contracts drawn up at the time will define the rights. However, a lot of low-budget productions cannot afford original music and therefore buy it 'off the shelf'. This means that permission has to be obtained to use it.

As was mentioned in the previous chapter the two organizations that have to be contacted are the Performing Rights Society (PRS) and the Mechanical Copyright Protection Society (MCPS). The PRS is engaged in the collection and distribution of the royalties payable for the use of copyrighted music. This means that if a production uses a piece of music by a composer whose work is still in copyright then it pays the PRS a sum of money for the use of the copyright. The PRS will then pay the composer. It does not matter who recorded the music, the composer still has to be paid. The PRS decides how much has to be paid and this figure will vary depending on the popularity of the particular composer and the use to which the music is put. The initial business of the MCPS is the clearance of recording copyrights on the music used in a film. This means, for instance, that although there may be no payment to Mozart, through the PRS, for the use of his music there will certainly be a payment to the orchestra or musicians for the use of their recording of Mozart's music and this will be done through the MCPS. Only where a composer is still in copyright will both societies have to be paid and the best way to find out the position is to contact both organizations during pre-production.

The next most likely area requiring clearances is if any library or archive footage is used. Like the PRS and MCPS, the individual libraries will quote their rates for the material required. The cost will depend on what the material is and how it is to be used. The eventual use of the footage will influence its cost, as will the amount of footage used. Usually it is offered on the basis of a minimum of a minute, or part thereof. This means that using the same piece twice constitutes two usages and results in two payments. The same is true if two separate sections, each of say 10 seconds duration, are used and even if they are only separated by 5 seconds they will count for two separate fees. As ever, the production manager must be sure of what the production is buying.

Generally speaking, because the backers want the film delivered without encumbrances, library footage is contracted for on the terms of 'all media and all territories'. The 'all media' part means the finished programme can be shown in cinema, on television by broadcast, cable, satellite or videotape or any other method yet to be invented. The 'all territories' part allows the programme to be shown anywhere in the universe. The use of the word universe may seem extreme but when one realizes that these days films are seen on aeroplanes one can only guess at the possible venues in the next century.

It should be obvious that it is easier to sort out these clearances as the film proceeds. This means that the production office should obtain and keep the evidence that the rights are in the hands of the production company. The logic of this action, as it has already been noted, is that it is easier than trying to catch up with artistes or individuals who have moved on to another job after finishing with the production. The other reason is that distant locations are not always easy to return to.

The one thing that should not be done is for the production to assume that the owner of a copyright that has not been cleared or a performer who has not signed a contract or rights waiver will not follow up with a later claim. Recently a film school delivered a number of short films to a television company for use on one of their programmes. One of the shorts had a performance by an actor who had not signed a release form. The actor's agent saw the programme with the result that almost all the money paid by the television company to the school was subsequently paid to the actor as a standard minimum performance fee. Consequently all the signed contracts and clearances should be properly filed, even after the delivery of the production.

Besides ensuring that the material is delivered without any legal or financial problems hanging over it there will be other conditions to be met. The most obvious of these is connected with publicizing the film.

PUBLICITY

Publicity is a major part of the production of a feature film and there have been times when more money has been spent on publicizing a film than on producing it in the first place although often to no advantage.

Regardless of the sums spent on publicity the production manager needs to be aware of publicity requirements. While the production is being shot on of the activities the producer will be involved in is the promotion of the film.

Although publicizing a film is usually the job of the distributor it cannot be done without the assistance of the production company. As already mentioned, during the shoot the press will be invited to visit the set or location and this has to be arranged in conjunction with the production office. In addition to these press and photo opportunities the production company will be obliged to provide photographs, or 'stills', for publicity.

Another publicity requirement will be a synopsis of the story and/or production notes on the film. These notes will comment on the director's interpretation of the story and will probably include any interesting tales which might help the production to get coverage in other areas of the media. Also, there may be contractual duties in the delivery requirements for the cast, director or other senior crew to be present at premières or other occasions, like film festivals, where publicity is to be generated.

This sort of activity will continue long after the film is delivered but usually is part of the contract for the production, so the material and information must be made available by the production office for these demands to be complied with. It is easier to gather this material as production progresses rather than collecting it at a later date.

This is equally true for delivery to television companies, although on a lesser scale. The programme will usually be delivered a month or more before the scheduled programme date so that a press showing can be arranged and the publicity distributed. This time is also needed to confirm that the programme has met its other contractual requirements and to receive formal approval from the broadcasting authorities. This latter approval relates to censorship.

FILM CENSORS

Before a film can be screened in the UK it has to receive a licence. In the early days of the industry individual councils issued licences but this soon proved to be far too difficult to operate. Each council had its own idea of what could be licensed and the level of censorship entered into what was intended to be approval for fire regulations. Some authorities found some parts of a film more inflammable than others and the result was that there was no consistency in the approval of films. A council might ban one film and accept another while its next-door neighbour did the complete opposite. The industry, in an effort to simplify matters, set up the British Board of Film Censors now known as the British Board of Film Classification (BBFC). This body issues a recommended certificate for a film and generally this is accepted by the local authorities as a whole. However, films can still be shown in Britain without a certificate if the local authority approves. This system is broadly followed in every country.

Thus, in the United States a film has to meet the approval of the Production Code which for a long time was known as the Hays Office, while other countries have their own systems. In any event, whatever the country, often a film cannot get a public screening without the appropriate certificate and sometimes there will be a debate between the producers and the certifiers or 'censors' about the certificate to be issued.

There are numerous stories in the industry about producers of horror films asking the censor to give the film an 'X' certificate because they feel the public will not go to a horror film with any lower rating. Equally, there have been films which have had some very strangely edited scenes in them because the censors objected to some dialogue or a shot and the only way the producer could have the film distributed with a lesser rating was by having the offending section cut from the film. The film *The Killing of Sister George* had a whole sequence in it shot without music in the expectation that the censors would ask for it be cut. They did not, and this resulted in some local councils reclaiming their right to censor films shown in cinemas under their control, so for a while this film could be seen in some parts of Britain but not in others. The incidental publicity did the film a lot of good at the box office.

For the production manager last minute changes can be very expensive, so, as ever, the solution is to let people know what is happening in good time. If the BBFC is aware of possible trouble in a picture before the editing is finished it can see the film while changes can be made without causing extra cost, rather than wait for later when a redub might be needed or later still when a whole new answer print could be called for.

PRINTS

This is a stage in which the production manager will not be involved, but an understanding is helpful. For a feature film to have a general release in Britain perhaps as many as 200 prints will have to be made. This will mean that two or more colour reversal internegatives (CRIs) will have to be made and from these the distribution prints will be struck. The laboratories will only know this if they receive proper instructions and these will probably come from the distributor. On the other hand, a programme made for television may meet delivery requirements with two video masters. Again the laboratory has to be instructed properly.

OTHER REQUIREMENTS

Individual contracts may have other delivery terms in them and it is only by being aware of the requirements that the production can be completed properly.

These terms may range from preparing material for a film festival to the managing of a première prior to general release.

Finally the backer will want an up-to-date account on the production and this will certainly be part of the delivery terms of the film.

ACCOUNTS

Every business is obliged to account for its activities and this is particularly true in an industry where vast sums of money are invested in the making of the product. Productions which are financed to the tune of £10 million or £20 million for the negative are obviously open to abuse. The temptation for people involved with this scale of production to think that no one will notice the loss of the odd thousand pounds here or there should be realized by the production staff.

For the most part crews are honest but, human nature being what it is, there is no guarantee that every one will be so. This is equally true from top executives, who have been known to forge cheques, down to the lowliest runners, who may try to fiddle their expenses or overtime.

Keeping track of the finances is vitally important and these days with the aid of computer accounting it is much easier. A production will buy a lot of props and other items or materials which rightly belong to the production company. With the aid of computers these things can now be kept track of, whereas in the past it would not have been worth the effort. Yet these items can be resold and on a tight budget this hidden cash can help bring the production in on budget.

Essentially the production accountant should keep track of details like these but in the final analysis it is the production manager who is accountable and who must ensure that the accounts are up to date.

The same applies to low-budget productions made for television, as the production fee will not be paid until the accounts are presented and agreed.

Therefore the efficient and competent production manager should keep in mind the business motto which states that 'The job isn't finished until the paperwork is done.' It is just as true for film production as any other industry.

CHAPTER 18

THE BUSINESS OF PRODUCTION

A film is the last travelling circus.
David Lean

If a film is the last travelling circus then the job of the production manager is that of the ring master. They are the people who arrange for the 'acts' to arrive punctually and economically. Essentially it is their job to ensure that the 'circus' runs smoothly.

In order to do this the production manager must understand the financial as well as the organizational aspects that have to be met in a production. In other words the production manager needs an understanding of the business of production.

It is not within the scope of this book to explore the entrepreneurial skills required by a producer but, as has been said before, the process of film making is a business and as with all businesses the intention is to make a profit. How the profit is made depends on the kind of production — feature or documentary, pop promo or commercial — and the terms that the producer negotiates for the financing of the film.

Also, there is the question of what the financiers want from the film and this is particularly true of feature productions, especially those made under the Hollywood system. In passing it is also important to understand the way Hollywood works and consequently what can or cannot be achieved when a major studio is approached. For example, no major studio will accept unsolicited feature scripts. The simple reason for this is that studios and producers all have projects in development. If they receive a script which is similar to a story they are already trying to raise money for, they do not wish to be sued by the prospective writer for breach of copyright when their own idea is produced. It may seem that they will lose some wonderful ideas but in fact a good script will surface more quickly through the hands of agents or other development agencies than if sent direct to a major financier.

A low-budget feature, in today's market, is accepted as being £1½ million pounds or less. Drama films made for television, which are usually

shot on 16 mm film rather than 35 mm, will usually fall into this category as they will expect to have a budget in the region of three-quarters
of a million, assuming no exceptional circumstances. An example of an
exceptional circumstance was a recent dramatization of a Charles Dick-
ens' novel for BBC Television where all the costumes were hand sewn,
an expensive business which was reflected in the eventual cost of the
production. Of course television drama is also shot on tape, but in terms
of eventual cost this choice will not necessarily result in a marked saving.

The financing of a feature film is a lengthy and complex business and
can be achieved in various ways. For the production manager the important fact is to get the film in on time and on budget so that the producer
can deliver it and meet the contractual obligations. Any problems in the
production resulting in late delivery or over-run in the budget will have
an effect on the profit.

The profit on a feature film is initially expected to come from the box
office returns at the cinema and a film which does badly at the cinema
can very quickly be in deep financial trouble, particularly when it is realized that, as a rule of thumb, for every unit of currency spent on the production at least four units have to be returned at the box office before a
film can begin to go into profit and sometimes, depending on how the
production was financed, the ratio can be 10 to 1 or more.

There are other factors which affect feature budgets and one of these
is the current money market, specifically the interest rate. A film with a
budget of £10 million has to pay interest on this money while it is being
used. It can take a year or more between signature of the contracts,
which means the handing over of the money, and the première or release
date, when the money hopefully begins to return. It should be obvious
that 15% say, on £10 million is a large part of a budget and any overspend simply means more money to be raised, usually at higher interest, and consequently more money to be earned before the production
breaks even. Therefore the more expensive the production the harder it
is to make a profit.

One of the ways a producer may work to guarantee a profit is to sell
the film as it is being made. Joseph E. Levene, while producing *A Bridge
Too Far*, worked in this way. By letting distributors see the partly made
film while it was being shot he managed to tie up distribution deals so
that the film was in profit before it was completed. However, it only
remained in profit because it was completed on time and under budget.

The understanding of why a film is made is also important. As has
been said earlier it is to do with money. An individual may have a pet
project but until the backers think they are going to get some financial
benefit from the production it will not get off the ground. The reason
why bad cheap movies are made is simply because they are cheap and
the investors think they will get a quick return on the product. Sometimes there are other reasons for investing in a film. An example of this
is the film *Sheena, Queen of the Jungle*. The level of this production can
be judged by the fact that in the film Sheena rode around on a zebra but,

because zebras are very hard to train, in reality it was a white horse painted with black stripes. The question asked by the discerning cinema goer is why did anyone give the producers the money in the first place? The answer in this particular instance was that at the time a well-known drinks company which owned the financing company had surplus finance in the country where the film was shot. The country's finance laws did not allow for the transfer of the surplus money out of the country. Consequently the drinks company instructed its film subsidiary to shoot a film financed by the surplus. Once the film was made the negative was taken out of the country. On every film the negative is valued at the total investment, but not everyone realizes this fact and in this instance x million dollars left the country in the form of the negative. Back in the United States the parent company billed their subsidiary for the money loaned by their African branch. So this film got made because financiers wanted to get money out of one country into another. This is an exception but it helps to understand why films might be financed.

The basic reason is that financing companies have agreements to provide films for the cinema circuit and therefore they must back independent productions or make films themselves in order to meet their commitments.

In the world of television the reasoning is similar. A television company has 18 hours or more a day, 52 weeks of the year, in which to provide programmes. Therefore it needs programme makers, either in-house or independents from outside.

For the independent production company the immediate profit is the production fee. This fee is usually a percentage of the agreed budget and, for example, the fee at Channel 4 Television Ltd is between 10% and 15% of the budget. This percentage is calculated on the size of the budget and is increased at accepted levels as the budget gets smaller. Thus a one-off half-hour minimal budget documentary will receive a 15% fee whereas a documentary series will receive a lesser percentage because the total budget is bigger, even if the individual budgets are the same.

However, should the production run over budget the additional cost comes out of this production fee and only if all the production fee is used up will negotiations commence about additional funding.

The production fee is paid to the commissioned production company, never to an individual, so if the company is to survive it cannot afford to run over budget otherwise the immediate profit is lost. A longer-term profit on a production may be gained from additional sales through other outlets in other countries or on other media, like videotape, but it should be realized that some films are too parochial for wider distribution. Documentaries about wildlife have worldwide appeal but a film about, say, the particular political and social problems of a specific community is unlikely to have appeal outside that area and therefore additional sales should not be expected.

If a film proves to have a wider sales potential then this should be dealt with by a distributor.

Some producers have the mistaken belief that they can sell their own film better than a distributor or distributor's agent. This may be true in terms of enthusiasm but is unlikely to be true in terms of economics. Suppose an hour-long documentary has been made about life in London's China Town; it might be sold to broadcast television for a price around £10 000 depending on the slot offered. If this same programme is taken to Hong Kong, which has a population one-tenth the size of the United Kingdom's, then the sort of price that may be offered will be a tenth of the UK price or about £1000. It will cost a producer more than this to get to the Hong Kong market but a distributor, with thirty, fifty or a hundred programmes to sell, is in a completely different position. The first four or five films sold will cover the expenses of the trip and after that every sale is towards profit. The other real advantage that a distributor has is a knowledge of the market and which market places, or film festivals, to go to.

Documentary films may have a potential world market but essentially they are only saleable to television. At the present time there are a number of different television formats throughout the world. The transfer of a videotape from the British television format to the US television format is an expensive business. Transferring from film to video is a far cheaper process and this is one reason why programmes are still shot on film even though they are aimed at the television market.

Other kinds of programme have their own outlets but if your proposal does not fit the kind of outlet you are approaching you will not get the finance to make your film.

Finally it needs to remembered that films are not made by one person and for a production to be successful a producer needs a good crew to do the filming, a good lawyer to deal with contracts, a good accountant to control the books and finance, a good insurance broker for insurance advice. If a feature is being planned the producer will also need a completion bond to ensure that the film is completed, a good clearance team who will be responsible for ensuring that the film can be sold anywhere and no one will make additional claims on the production, and finally a good publicist so that everyone knows the film has been made.

At the beginning of this book the point was made that there are no golden rules in the business of production management. The producing of a film has none of the certainties that camera technicians have about the focal length of lenses or sound recordists have about the amplitude of sound waves. However, if there is one lesson that should be learnt by production crews and production managers in particular it is the need to keep everyone informed. No one can know too much about what is supposed to be happening and what is really happening. It is only from full information that correct actions can be taken and only when the correct decisions are made will the production run smoothly.

It is hoped that this book will help your productions to run more smoothly.

INDEX